Those Vulgar Tube

A complete listing of books
in print in this series appears on the last page.

Those Vulgar Tubes

External Sanitary Accommodations aboard European Ships
of the Fifteenth through Seventeenth Centuries

Second Edition

by
JOE J. SIMMONS III

Texas A&M University Press
College Station

CHATHAM PUBLISHING

LONDON

Copyright © 1997 by Joe J. Simmons III
Manufactured in the United States of America
All rights reserved
First Texas A&M University Press edition
04 03 02 01 00 99 98 97   5 4 3 2 1

First published in 1991 by the Nautical Archaeology Program,
Department of Anthropology, Texas A&M University

Published in Great Britain in 1998 by
    Chatham Publishing
    1 & 2 Faulkner's Alley
    Cowcross Street
    London ECIM 6DD
    Chatham Publishing is an imprint of
    Gerald Duckworth & Co Ltd

Main title adapted from a poem attributed to William Falconer, entitled
"A Sea Chaplain's Petition to the Lieutenants in the Ward Room,
for the Use of the Quarter Gallery." *Gentleman's Magazine* 28 (August 1758): 371.

Figure 6.2 art by David Macaulay; all other drawings by the author.

The paper used in this book meets the minimum requirements of the American
National Standard for Permanence of Paper for Printed Library Materials,
Z39.48-1984. Binding materials have been chosen for durability.

Library of Congress Cataloging-in-Publication Data

Simmons, Joe J.
        Those vulgar tubes : external sanitary accommodations aboard European
    ships of the fifteenth through seventeenth centuries / Joe J. Simmons III.
    — 2nd ed.
            p.   cm. — (Studies in nautical archaeology ; no. 1)
        Includes bibliographical references and index.
        ISBN 0-89096-788-1
        1. Ships—Sanitation—History. I. Title. II. Series.
    VM481.S56   1998
    623.8′546—dc21   97-25423
                                                                    CIP

British Library Cataloging in Publication Data
Acatalogue record for this book is available from the British Library
Chatham ISBN 1-86176-043-4

To All Those Who Have Gone at Sea

Contents

Illustrations

Acknowledgments

I am grateful for the aid and encouragement of numerous kind souls during the inception and production of this work. What began as a term paper for a course offered by J. Richard Steffy on the history of ship construction was substantially focused and transformed into a master's thesis, largely at his urging. Thanks, Dick. The other members of my committee, chaired by George F. Bass, were no less instrumental in the completion of my course of study.

The scatological subject matter herein naturally lends itself to a rather tongue-in-cheek approach; I am appreciative of those who laughed with me yet saw the more serious and, it is hoped, contributive aspects of the investigation . . . you know who you are. Thanks are due to those friends and colleagues (the two not being mutually exclusive) who supplied me with juicy tidbits regarding the more basic qualities of shipboard life.

My sincerest thanks to David Macaulay for contributing the art for figure 6.2, especially on such short notice.

Former *Studies in Nautical Archaeology* series general editor Michael Fitzgerald was extremely helpful and, indeed, was the driving force behind the initial publication of this monograph. Nevertheless, all sins of omission and commission are entirely my own.

Those Vulgar Tubes

Introduction 1

The disposal of human wastes generated aboard ships has been an important consideration throughout the roughly ten thousand–year history of navigation and remains so to this day. It certainly has been no less crucial to health maintenance than the proper disposal of human excreta from terrestrial habitation sites. It is therefore rather surprising that, with few exceptions, the issue has been excluded from the literary and representational corpus.

Societal and cultural mores and strictures, a modest hesitation to describe or depict the performance of such common, basic bodily functions, and the possible censorship of edited contemporary accounts offer the best explanations for the lack of contemporary information. These same factors may also explain the reluctance of modern historians to deal directly with methods of human waste removal, the conditions that improper disposal precipitated, and the structural modifications made to vessels to facilitate removal. It remains certain, however, that, despite an apparent aversion on the part of writers and artists to address the subject, it demanded attention whenever and wherever men took to the sea.

To gain a better understanding of what life aboard ships was like during the fifteenth through seventeenth centuries, it is clear that a more complete analysis of human waste disposal at sea is in order. The objective is to examine the development of the "heads," "round-houses," "quarter galleries," and other structural features designed or used to facilitate the removal of human waste aboard European ships of the period. Analogous or similar features on vessels prior to this period that could have served as conveniences are surveyed, and de-

vices that continued to be used into the nineteenth century are re-
viewed as well.

According to the technologies of a particular period, easily por-
table collection containers of wood, ceramic, or metal were quite common aboard all vessels, and such nonstructural appliances (e.g., wooden
waste buckets and ceramic or metal chamber pots) were used on board
sailing vessels throughout the age of sail. Chamber pots were probably employed more often by officers and privileged passengers than
by members of the crew, who used the cruder forms of collection
containers. Chamber pots are often found among the remains of "old
wooden shipwrecks," such as that of the *Hollandia*, which came to
grief off the Isles of Scilly in 1743, and another in the Bay of Cadiz,
Spain, thought to have sunk in 1805 after the Battle of Trafalgar.[1]
These containers were used in addition to the external accommodations of any given vessel and were relied upon heavily during weather
too rough to permit access to the external facilities (if such existed) or
when a large portion of the complement was incapacitated by sickness. As recently as 1875, the formal sanitary removal scheme in British steam-gunboats consisted of "bucket and screen" for the ship's
company.[2]

Early Evidence of Human Waste Removal from Watercraft

Because of their very nature, waterborne craft have usually been "able
to accommodate the human need."[3] By simply eliminating excreta
directly into the sea or by throwing collected materials overboard,
shipboard occupants established an efficient, common-sense disposal
scheme. Prior to the fifteenth century, such rudimentary methods of
waste removal were undoubtedly in use on most vessels and, as situa-
tions warranted, they certainly persisted from the fifteenth century
until the end of the age of sail.

In what were usually relatively small, undecked, or partly decked
vessels that were limited to coastal, lacustrine, and riverine areas and
that made no voyages longer than one or two days without landing,
there was no need for anything more elaborate than waste buckets or
a small platform from which to answer the call of nature. Such a platform could have been the gunwale or perhaps a device fastened to the
exterior of the hull. In a maritime scene painted on a Cypriot pitcher
dated to the seventh century B.C., a sailor is rather graphically shown
relieving himself from what is apparently the quarter rudder at the
stern of the vessel; a fish is partaking of this bounty from above.[4]

The hypothesized functions of a unique attachment on the sterns of several ships painstakingly depicted in a fresco that seems to date to the later seventeenth century B.C. (Fig. 1.1), unearthed on the island of Santorini (ancient Thera), include that of a lavatory for crew or officers.[5] As the devices seem to have been mounted either at or very near the waterline, their use under any but ideal sea conditions would have been hazardous, to say the least, and access would seem to have been difficult.

Indeed, the idea would hardly be worthy of consideration were it not for an intriguing depiction on an ivory plaque from Sparta that dates to perhaps one thousand years later (Fig. 1.2). The realistic representation of a Greek warship of around 600 B.C. includes a man who

Fig. 1.1. Thera ship with stern appendage, seventeenth century B.C. (After Marinatos 1974: 48, fig. 5.)

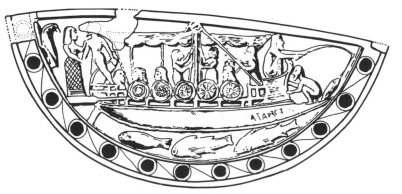

Fig. 1.2. Ivory plaque from the sanctuary of Artemis Orthia, Sparta, ca. 600 B.C. (After DeVries and Katzev 1972: 42, fig. 5.)

is crouched on the ramlike projection of the vessel and is engaged
either in a particularly degrading form of contrition or in eliminating
his bowels.[6] The latter seems far more plausible; one shipmate even
seems to be taking advantage of the situation by angling in the "baited"
water. However, this use of the ramlike structure would bear the same
disadvantages noted for the stern appendages of the Thera ships. Although access may have been somewhat improved, it still would have
been a fair-weather accommodation.

It should be noted that, in representations of some Roman merchant ships, the stern-most extremity of the deck appears to be covered.[7] Some suggest that this was a place where the ship's officers and
perhaps important passengers could answer the call of nature.[8]

The earliest literary reference found that appears to relate specifically to the collection and removal of human wastes aboard ships
is in the form of a purchase order for one thousand *ptuaria* (little
spitters)—waste buckets—for a fleet of twenty Byzantine dromons in
A.D. 949. Each dromon had a crew of approximately two hundred,
which suggests that each waste bucket was to be shared by four men,
perhaps a standard crew subunit.[9]

Conditions aboard Later Ships

In the course of the thirteenth and fourteenth centuries, as compasses
and nautical charts were developed and watercraft that could withstand the rigors of sustained and repeated deepwater navigation were
evolving, unique sanitary and hygienic problems appeared. Foremost
among these were removing human wastes efficiently; living healthfully
in what were characteristically filthy, damp, and usually crowded conditions; caring for the sick and injured on board ship; and provision-
ing. (The latter two issues are beyond the scope of this book.)

Internal structural configurations of the ships were responsible,
at least in part, for a great deal of discomfort and death. As vessels
began to be decked over, which improved their seaworthiness and
offered more protection from the elements, several factors combined
to compromise these benefits: diminished air flow to spaces between
and below decks, decreased light at lower deck levels, and accord-
ingly, higher humidity below decks.

Of overriding importance is the fact that the "stacking up" of
living surfaces, one above another, created a birdcage-like environment in which every imaginable bit of debris, filth, and human effluvia from the decks above gravitated to the bilges below. By the fifteenth

century, multiple decks were quite common in the largest types of vessels. Yet even smaller ships of the period, such as caravels, with only one or two deck levels aft, harbored unhealthy conditions within.

Multidecked ships generally had such features as waterways and scuppers to aid drainage to the exterior of the vessel. But faulty or poorly fitted scuppers and loose caulking between deck planks and along waterways allowed downward drainage through the decks of the vessel to the hold, ballast, and bilges. In addition, passengers and crew unable to relieve themselves at external sanitary facilities, or to empty the collection buckets' contents overboard during inclement weather, or who were too sick to move were often forced to eliminate bodily wastes within the confines of the hull. The consequent accumulation constituted a rich organic compost in the lowest, stygian reaches of the ships.

When conditions below decks became unbearable and started emitting "pestilential funkes," it was necessary to "rummage" the ship. In the sixteenth century, this consisted of "heaving her down on some convenient beach, throwing all ballast overboard so that the tide would cleanse it, scraping the horrible gunk off the inside of the hold, spraying it with vinegar, and replacing the ballast with clean stones, sand or shingle."[10] In later years, carbolic acid, iron sulfate, bichloride of mercury, and other chemical cleansing and disinfecting agents were employed.[11]

The size of individual ballast elements—whether sand, pebbles, cobbles, large stones, or metal objects—was also a factor that determined the relative nastiness of the bilges. The smaller the ballast objects, the greater the surface area available for the growth of algae, fungi, and bacteria. A gradual increase in the preferred size of ballast is evident from an examination of practices of the British navy. Until about 1600, sand was employed extensively, in addition to pebble-sized gravel or "shingle," cobblestones, and in some instances, lead ingots. But during the seventeenth century, ballast size was progressively increased to ease handling. This in turn afforded better aeration and decreased the surface area available for fungal and bacterial growth. It also must have reduced the clogging of limber holes and watercourses, while diminishing the adverse effects of sand on the pumps. Lead ingots continued to be used, and broken pieces of iron cannon, anchors, and outsized shot, for instance, were frequently used as ballast, in concert with stone.[12] Permanent pig-iron ballast, cast in stackable shapes, apparently made its appearance in the first half of the eighteenth century.[13]

Presumably, similar attempts to improve the dreadful conditions in the bilges were undertaken by other European navies and merchant fleets. However, a peculiar practice of at least two European navies probably negated any improvements that an increase in the size of ballast objects or any other hygienic measures would have afforded: the Catholic concept of consecrated burial ground and the dictates of canonical law prescribed against French and Iberian mariners' disposing of their dead at sea. As late as 1780, French ships captured during Rodney's campaign in the West Indies were observed to be carrying mangled limbs and decomposing corpses in the ballast.[14] Could the human skull found between the floor timbers of the wreck of the *St. Joseph*, a member of the ill-fated 1733 Spanish fleet, represent someone buried in the ballast, rather than a victim of the wreck or a drowned salvage diver, as supposed?[15]

Of course, not every ship's company felt so bound by the prescription against burial at sea. The many who died on Vasco da Gama's first voyage to India in 1497 were thrown overboard with striking frequency, perhaps indicating that, in this case at least, pragmatism won out over religious dictates.[16]

Pumps were of some help in improving conditions in the bilges. They were usually set low in the hull next to the keelson in a recess or well, to which the bilge water could run. This flow of water was unhindered by the framing of the hull due to the cutting of limber holes and/or watercourses into the underside of each frame. From time to time, however, these became clogged with the finer bits of debris and denser organic materials that worked their way down through the ballast to the lowest reaches of the ship. When this occurred it was necessary to break up the obstructions, so limber ropes or, to coin a term, "limber floss," which passed through the limber holes along the keel or the watercourses farther from the keel, were pulled back and forth.[17] In fact, such a simple concept is known from Roman times.[18]

In 1689, the sickness and foul conditions on board the *Dartmouth*, a British fifth-rate, were so bad that the ballast and bilge, "stinking and all of a quagmire," prevented the water from flowing into the pump wells. It seems that the ship was not equipped with limber floss; otherwise it would have been used. "Had we that ballast out, and [clean] shingle in," noted the *Dartmouth*'s lieutenant, "I doubt not but our ship would be healthy and in good condition."[19]

Archaeological evidence for the nature of bilges during the seventeenth century has been obtained from two wrecks. The *Sea Ven-*

ture, lost in 1607 off Bermuda, was found to contain a rich organic layer just above the bottom-most portion of the hull remains. Although it is not known if this deposit was thoroughly analyzed, it was tentatively identified as being composed partly of fecal materials.[20] On the wreck site of the *Kennemerland*, a Dutch East Indiaman that wrecked in the British Isles in 1664, a layer of matted organic remains consisting of wood splinters, patches of wood tar, resin, coal, seeds, peppercorns, pieces of leather, fragments of oakum and rope, and other artifacts was noted in at least two different areas of the site. This was assumed to constitute an undisturbed seventeenth-century horizon that probably originated in the bilges of the *Kennemerland*. In fact, when recovered from the site, a sample was said to have "smelt strongly like the contents of any wooden boat's bilges."[21]

When ships leaked, as ships from all periods have been prone to do, or when they had accumulated too much rainwater, wave splash, barrel leakages, and sundry contributions from passengers and crew, the pumps were employed to bring the mixture of thriving organic residue to one of the upper deck levels. Here it was discharged onto the deck in order to exit the vessel through the scuppers or to flow into troughs, called dales, which channeled the discharge closer to the scuppers. By all accounts, the resulting smell was overwhelming. A Franciscan friar traveling from Spain to Mexico in 1544 with Bishop Bartolome de las Casas was greatly offended by what issued from the pumps of his ship: "The air is foul, especially below decks, and intolerable throughout the ship when the pumps are going, and these work more or less frequently, depending on whether it is a good or a bad ship. The least they pump is four or five times a day, in order to drain out the water that leaks into the ship, and this bilge water stinks."[22]

Eugenio de Salazar, traveling to the New World in 1573 on a moderate-sized, 120-ton vessel, described the workings of the pumps during his five weeks on board. In a letter home he stated that the ship had "one or two fountains, called pumps, that water from which [was] unfit for tongue and palate to taste, or nostrils to smell, or even eyes to see, for it comes out bubbling like Hell and stinking like the Devil." He added that the pump-dales were "running rivers, not of sweet, clear, flowing water, but of turbid filth: full not of grains of gold like the Cibao or the Tagus, but of grains of very singular pearl—enormous lice, so big, that sometimes they are seasick and vomit bits of apprentice." In addition, Salazar noted that inside the vessel it was "closed-in, dark, and evil-smelling," and it reminded him of "burial vaults or charnel houses."[23] This scathing testimony falls far short of an endorsement of transatlantic travel in the period.

Conditions aboard ships did not improve much, if any, in the seventeenth century, even though, by external appearances, the prolific ornamentation and decoration of vessels of this century bespoke a certain enlightenment. The ships remained "cramped, uncomfortable, and filthy places for human beings to live. Sanitary facilities were entirely inadequate. With hundreds of men living in close proximity, the ships were breeding places for all sorts of infectious diseases . . . and mortality rates of 15% per year were not looked upon as especially bad."[24]

Nor was there any improvement in the eighteenth century. In fact, during this time the practice of purposeful overmanning peaked and greatly aggravated the poor conditions that already existed. Overmanning meant signing on more men than were necessary to sail and defend the ships, so that, when sickness and injury incapacitated crewmen, there were others to take their places. This is an excellent example of a deadly catch-22 cycle that, once established, frequently spelled the difference between the successful completion of a voyage or campaign and utter disaster for crew and vessel.

Understandably, rough weather only worsened the hygienic situation. First-time voyagers or those susceptible to seasickness were particularly disadvantaged by storms at sea. The unfortunate Franciscan of 1544 was a first-timer when his ship encountered a tempest in the tropics: "Shortly, the sea made us understand that it was no place for human habitation, and all of us collapsed as dead with seasickness. . . . Only the Father Vicar helped us, and placed basins and buckets for us to vomit in, which were of no use if they were not close at hand."[25]

The loss of the *Amsterdam* might be an example of the consequences of the complete incapacitation of a ship's complement. Sickness stemming from prolonged storm exposure in the North Sea in January is thought to have rendered the crew of the ship incapable of preventing it from going aground near Hastings in 1749.[26]

As a direct consequence of the fetid conditions between and below decks, and in the ballast and bilges especially, great numbers of vermin were able to breed and multiply virtually unchecked. Rats, lice, weevils, fleas, and cockroaches, to name a few, abounded. Rats were often found in such numbers that they became a supplement to the routine diet. During the first Pacific Ocean crossing in 1521, rats aboard vessels of Magellan's expedition were sold for six month's wages.[27] Landfall on the west coast of America during Cook's last voyage was celebrated by the "gentlemen of the gun room dining on a fricasse of rats."[28]

The importance of proper or, as was more often the case, improper waste-disposal schemes on board naval and merchant sailing vessels, which were, in effect, closed communities, cannot be overemphasized. Conscious attempts to improve the unhealthy interior conditions resulted in the development of external waste-disposal accommodations. It seems that any amount of bodily eliminations directed immediately into the sea, rather than to the interior of the hull, was regarded as advantageous at least in terms of sight and smell, even if the connection between filth and disease was not understood.

But even though the appearance and development of external waste-removal devices are readily observable in the pictorial record, their true efficacy is much more difficult to discern. Simply because such appliances were developed does not mean that sailors suddenly became "cleaner" or were more concerned with what are considered today to be acceptable hygienic standards. Moreover, their land-based contemporaries had no better understanding of the inseparable associations between filth and disease than did sailors. So conditions aboard sailing ships remained abominable, but it is not difficult to imagine what conditions would have been like if there had been no conscious attempts to deposit human effluvia directly overboard. Any efforts to ameliorate the situation, though seemingly ineffectual to us today, did in fact result in significant hygienic improvements.

The development of external sanitary conveniences can be shown to have been expedited by specific changes in northern European hull construction that occurred in the fifteenth, sixteenth, and seventeenth centuries. By the last quarter of the seventeenth century, these features were fully developed and most of them were retained with little or no modification until the early nineteenth century.

2

The Fifteenth Century

To understand the changes in hull construction that fostered the development of external sanitary accommodations on fifteenth-century vessels, a review of the trends in construction during the preceding two centuries is in order. Basically, external hygienic facilities were made possible by the construction of platforms at bow and stern that consisted of overhangs and projections, on which were erected devices that emptied directly into the sea. The following discussion primarily concerns the larger types of ships of the period: carracks, naos, hulks, and cogs. When no distinction is made, generalizations for ships of the period are intended.

Pre-Fifteenth-Century Bow and Stern Evolution

From double-ended ships that had small, lightweight platforms or decking added at either or both ends, the typical sailing ships of the thirteenth and fourteenth centuries evolved by the fifteenth century into vessels with distinct, characteristic built-up features in the bow and stern.

In the twelfth and thirteenth centuries, stages, or "castles," which were essentially temporary fighting platforms, were located at either end of the simple, double-ended hull. Named castles for good reason, these platforms incorporated features of contemporary terrestrial military architecture (e.g., battlements) because of the similar tactics used on land and sea at the time. A battle at sea was simply a land engagement fought on floating platforms, with comparable styles of attack and defense. "Warships had high sides—the equivalent of castle walls—and the high stages at bow and stern provided command and enfilading fire as a castle's towers did."[1] Castles on vessels of this period were still quite lightly built, in contrast to the much stouter, more castlelike structures developed in the fifteenth century.

As early as 1150, stages, or *bellatoria*, are shown erected on stanchions in the sterns of northern European ships. Late in the twelfth century, raised platforms appear at the bow.[2] City seals of the thirteenth century display square or polygonal platforms standing independently of the stem and sternpost, on wooden stanchions (Fig. 2.1). Apparently these platforms were fixed to the upper deck and planking. But during this century the stages were moved toward the fore and after extremities, where the stem and sternpost could be used as supports. Subsequently, the stages were extended beyond the ends of the ships, leaving the stem and sternpost heads to rise uselessly through the middle of the platforms.[3]

The planar shapes of the bow stages are difficult to determine

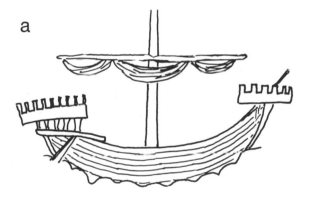

Fig. 2.1. Double-ended vessels with platforms at bow and stern, late thirteenth century. (A) (After Crumlin-Pedersen 1972: 199, ill. 20.) (B) (After Crumlin-Pedersen 1972: 196, ill. 13.)

with any confidence, but they tended to be of square, rectangular, and pentagonal configurations. By the late fourteenth century, the forward extremity of the forecastle had developed a distinct point. As the structure grew aft to occupy the entire space available in the bow, it assumed a triangular shape in plan that is in evidence throughout the greater part of the fifteenth century.[4]

With the replacement of quarter rudders by the stern rudder, the sternpost head was cut off to allow the tiller attached to the rudder head to operate properly. As a result, by the mid-fourteenth century, "the stern-castle, now unsupported by the sternpost, was modified in shape, becoming lower and longer than the fore-castle which, before, it had strongly resembled."[5] Drawing support for these structures from the fore and after portions of the hull and its framing made subsequent enlargements and elaborations possible.

A Hanse cog of around 1380 discovered in the Bremen harbor basin in 1962, while from northern Europe, bears out Nance's comments regarding the form of sterncastles by the mid-fourteenth century. It is indeed low, with only one level of two cabins beneath, and extends forward from just aft of the sternpost for more than one-third of the ship's length.[6] But more interesting is evidence for an actual stern-mounted hygienic accommodation (Fig. 2.2). The device, consisting of a simple wooden box with a keyhole-shaped opening in the seat, was secured to a portion of the main or castle deck that projected out from the starboard quarter. Thus positioned, the users, probably only the ship's officers, faced obliquely inboard toward the cabins when seated on the device and were afforded a modest degree of privacy.[7]

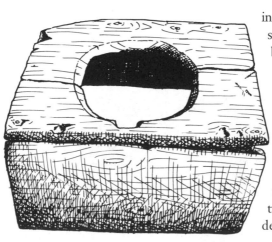

Fig. 2.2. Toilet box from the Bremen cog, ca. 1380. (After Kiedel 1985: 78, ill. 67.)

The emergence and incorporation of superstructures into the bow and stern apparently proceeded at a quicker pace in Mediterranean ships than in those of northern Europe during the fourteenth century.[8] The former were carrying two decks aft (quarter deck and poop deck) above the hull proper, while the quarter deck was still a novelty in England in the fourteenth century. Above the rounded sterns, the after ends of the overhanging decks terminated in a "square vertical bulwark." The projecting ends of these decks were supported by concave "counters," the framing of which was within the fabric of the hull.[9] The whole presented a rather boxlike appearance; Nance notes that "the idea of a rectangular 'castle,' added after the ship proper was built, evidently died hard."[10]

It has been suggested that the relatively elaborate stern structures in some southern, or "Latin," ship depictions of the fourteenth century, with their multiple, vertically rising stages and rudimentary side galleries, were directly influenced by the "higher, fuller stern[s] of Roman or earlier vessels."[11]

By the beginning of the fifteenth century, then, a prominent forward-projecting forecastle and boxlike after castle with an overhang at the stern and concave counter was the norm. Both superstructures were relatively lightly built and, although primarily erected on the external planking of the hull and the underlying decks at bow and stern, they were beginning to be integrated into the vessels' structural framing.

The Bow

As noted, the predominant shape of the forecastle on the larger ships of the fifteenth century, carracks especially, was triangular in plan view, with the apex of the triangle forward. But contemporary artists have left precious little evidence for the exact nature of the construction of forecastles on these vessels. A particularly informative depiction, dated to about 1450, is seen in figure 2.3A. The bow-on view clearly shows the underside of the triangular platform of the forestage, with its single longitudinal support, four transverse timbers, and what appears to be obliquely laid floor planking (cf. Fig. 2.3B). The space between the underside of the forestage and the carvel-built hull of this Mediterranean carrack is covered with diagonal clinker planking. Carracks of northern Europe had clinker planking that characteristically followed the line of the sheer in this space.[12] It was in this area that the incorporation of the forecastle into the hull was gradually effected.

This bow configuration changed very little during the fifteenth century. One alteration consisted of the addition of one or two levels to the height of the forestage, which by this time had attained dimensions sufficient for it to be termed a true fore-"castle," and no longer

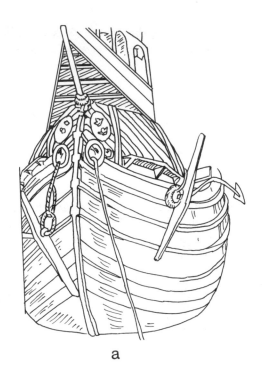

a

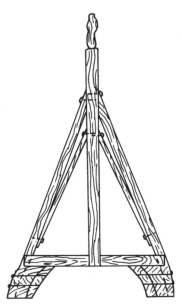

Fig. 2.3. Bow and forestage framework of fifteenth-century carracks. (A) Bow of carrack in Carpaccio's Legend of St. Ursula, *ca. 1450. (After Nance 1955a: 191, fig. 9.) (B) Framework of a fifteenth-century carrack's forestage from above. (After Howard 1979: 22, fig. 19.)*

b

a forestage, or more lightly built platform. Other modifications included the hyperextension of the forecastle forward and, during the last quarter of the century, the upper levels of the forecastle being supported by curved, rather than straight, stanchions.[13] By the end of the fifteenth century, further consolidation had occurred in both the bow and stern, "leaving traces of the stanchions on which they were formerly reared, in the tiers of arched openings which [served] to give light and to act as emplacements for swivel guns." Thus, vessels with the "towering poops and forecastles to which our eyes are accustomed in ships of the 16th century" had been developed.[14]

Unfortunately, neither these nor any other depictions, models, or contemporary accounts have yielded any incontrovertible evidence of what type of sanitary accommodations, if any, existed in the forecastles of vessels of this period. Logically, it would have been a simple matter not to lay floor planking over limited portions of the forecastle platform. Sections of planks could have been left out or replaced with wooden gratings, which were used as sanitary accommodations in the forward-projecting "beakheads" of ships throughout most of the sixteenth century. Slotlike defensive openings, or machicolations in medieval architectural parlance, were probably left in the projecting flooring at the bow. These openings could have easily served a hygienic function, as they certainly did in their terrestrial analogues. The striking similarities between defensive and sanitary features of castles and ships are further illustrated through an examination of the sterns of fifteenth-century vessels.

The Stern

Little change in the general stern configuration took place in the fifteenth century. The multiple, lightly built stages and tilt-frames, or awning supports, were gradually strengthened and further incorporated into the hull fabric and framing. Above the concave counter, most superstructures of the period were rectilinear and squared off, and the line from the counter to the upper rail of the sterncastle was vertical. By about 1450, the sternpost had become vertical, or nearly so, as well. The addition of the lower wing-transom below the tiller hole produced "what became the normal stern of the typical fifteenth-century carrack."[15] The "square tuck," or rectilinear, as opposed to rounded, hull shape in the stern area was introduced at the end of the century. In addition to making the placement of stern chase guns possible, the square tuck reduced the sheer in the stern while increasing the width of the extreme after end of the hull. This provided a more substantial base upon which to erect the stern superstructure and improved the ability of the counter to support upper works that were tending toward accentuated rake aft and multiple counters.[16]

In various depictions from the period, a number of features with obvious hygienic functions are evident at the sterns of vessels. Without doubt, the single best representation of the after end of a ship (in this case, a carrack) with such features is the *Kraeck* by the master WA (Fig. 2.4), a Flemish artist of the fifteenth century known for a series of detailed ship engravings. Evident in this depiction dated around 1470, and others to be presented, are the following: barrel-like attachments on the stern quarters and above the transom and counter,

Fig. 2.4. Detail of the master WA's Kraeck, *ca. 1470. (Reprinted by permission of the Ashmolean Museum, Oxford.)*

often called "steep-tubs," after a function of similar barrels; closetlike additions over the counters that project out from the sterncastle, similar to garderobes in contemporary castle architecture; structures that closely resemble castle turrets and that probably performed much the same function; and small projections through the counters that may have been "soil-pipes," or plumbing from sanitary facilities within the sterncastle.

STEEP-TUBS. Steep-tubs were wooden barrels, or half-barrels, generally understood to have been used to steep, or humidify and partly desalinate, salted meats—a staple for crews of sailing ships from at least as early as the fourteenth century to well into the nineteenth century.[17] An alternative function has been suggested as well: that of external sanitary accommodations.[18] One would hope that this dual purpose was not served by the same steep-tubs, but the modern and contemporary evidence, at least for the fifteenth century, is confusing, possibly due to application of the same or similar terms to both devices. Nevertheless, in illustrations from the fifteenth to the eighteenth centuries, they are depicted lashed upright to the stern quarters, directly aft over the counter, or in the mizzen or main chains. Barrels mounted horizontally in illustrations by WA and others are thought to have been associated with the fishing industry.

During the fifteenth century, steep-tubs were most commonly shown on the quarters and sterns of northern and southern vessels, with some distinction evident between the features of ships representative of the north as opposed to the south. WA's *Kraeck*, supposedly a Flemish carrack, has a steep-tub lashed to the port stern quarter just aft of the main chains, and presumably there was a corresponding one to starboard. The stern of another carrack drawn by WA is shown in figure 2.5. Two steep-tubs are depicted, one on each quarter, as are

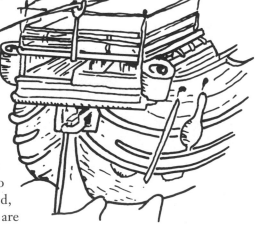

Fig. 2.5. Stern of a vessel illustrated by the master WA, ca. 1470. (After Nance 1955b: 282, fig. 12b.)

two unidentified objects on the starboard quarter. In addition, a partitioned, stall-like stern gallery with one large and two small enclosures is located directly aft, above the counter.

Representations of southern ships of this century (Fig. 2.6) often include a slightly different type of container lashed to the stern or fitted to a projecting ledge above the counter. Such containers seem to resemble large oil, water, or wine storage jars more than barrels, but the distinction is difficult to make. The jars "can hardly be 'steep-tubs,' such as WA would give his [northern] vessels, for in some instances we seem to have upon the quarter these same tubs for de-salting preserved meat as well as the objects astern."[19] Indeed, they were probably examples of some of the earliest external sanitary accommodations. Between the jarlike containers shown on these vessels, some interesting structures are depicted that appear to be large "hen coops" or small cratelike galleries, roughly similar to the small stalls on the stern of the ship in figure 2.5. Nance adds that these "crates . . . and the jars may be peculiarly southern equipage."[20]

An ethnological analogy can be drawn between these jars, barrels, hen coops, crates, and small boxlike galleries on fifteenth-century ships and the "sanitary boxes" of modern Arab *dhows*, *booms* (Fig. 2.7), *abubuzes*, and other vessels that have remained virtually unchanged for hundreds of years. Generally, sanitary boxes were "one-holed privies hung overboard off the poop, usually on the port side, but sometimes seen on starboard. . . . [They] usually lack the privacy of a privy, and are almost completely open."[21]

It is widely accepted that Arab influences on southern and, in

Fig. 2.6. Sterns of southern ships, late fifteenth century. (A, B) (After Howard 1979: 22, fig. 21.) (C) (After Howard 1979: 22, fig. 20.)

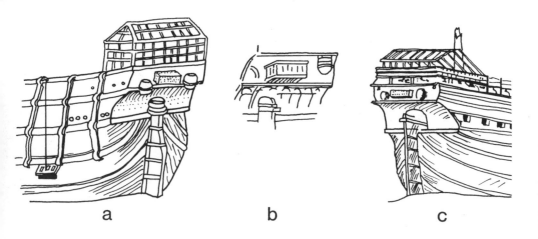

a   b   c

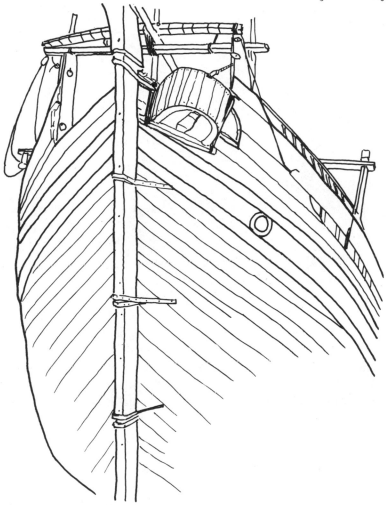

Fig. 2.7. Stern of an "80-year-old" boom *with sanitary box starboard of sternpost. (After Howarth 1977: 29.)*

turn, northern European ships, in terms of style, construction, and rigging, were substantial; certainly the adoption of one more feature is not implausible, especially if it offered distinct, readily apparent advantages.

Sanitary boxes were predominantly semicircular or square in plan view. Some were decorated or built with manifest artistry, but most were usually constructed in the plain, utilitarian fashion of a crate (Figs. 2.7, 2.8). Figure 2.8 is a detailed view of the interior of such a device; the most apparent feature, apart from the rough but well-made semicircular box itself, is the elongated keyhole-shaped slot in the

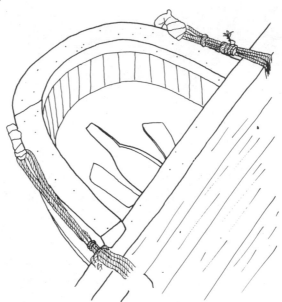

*Fig. 2.8. Interior
view of semicircular
sanitary box.
(After Howarth
1977: 55.)*

floor and the footpads on either side. Their alignment indicates that
the user would face outboard while squatting, feet placed on the pads.
Being simply lashed to the gunwale, such boxes could have been moved
easily from side to side as necessary, after changing tack.

The overwhelming simplicity and indisputable utility of such devices favor extreme conservatism in their use. In fact, it seems likely
that artists of the fifteenth century were attempting, in at least some
of their works, to depict external sanitary accommodations that were
quite comparable to modern Arab sanitary boxes. Interestingly, it has
been stated that Vasco da Gama's caravels of 1497, relatively small but
important ships of the period, were probably equipped with very similar
facilities. "For jakes there were the 'gardens,' stools hung over the
leeside, where, as like as not, the sweep of the water as the ship heeled
would wash your arse."[22]

GARDEROBES. In several interesting depictions from the fifteenth
century, most notably the *Kraeck* by WA (see Fig. 2.4), peculiar
closetlike additions project aft from the stern of the vessel, over the
counter. Here, two such structures are visible, one on each side of a
small, ballustraded gallery. The three sides of each are pierced with
what seem to be windows, presumably to admit light and afford some
ventilation. On the underside of each structure, part of the flooring

between the curved supports is missing, and below this, on the curved counter, small "shields" are evident. Between the additions are what have been interpreted as three doorways with round windows above them, or the artist's attempt to depict a trio of humans, possibly saints.[23]

These stern additions are so similar to the garderobes of medieval castle architecture that there can be little doubt about their intended use. Harris and Lever define a garderobe as a "euphemism for a privy in a medieval castle . . . [that] was built either within the thickness of the castle wall, or else projecting beyond the wall . . . [and draining] into the moat or into a special pit."[24] Obviously, access to the garderobes was from the interior of the castle. Thompson, in his *Military Architecture in Medieval England*, has further characterized these terrestrial hygienic facilities: "the outer wall, in which the seat was contained, was slightly thickened and corbelled out at this level, and a vent made below the seat."[25] Garderobes were usually equipped with a loop or slot in the masonry to allow the entrance of air and light.[26] Figure 2.9 illustrates the classic type of garderobe constructed in medieval European castles. They could have served as excellent models for their maritime counterparts.

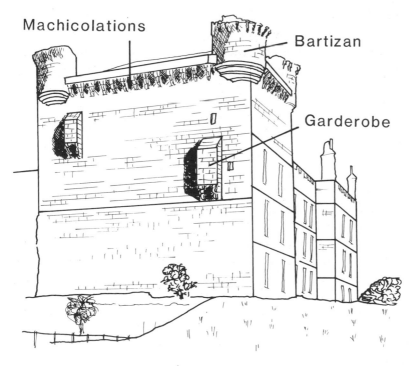

Machicolations

Bartizan

Garderobe

Fig. 2.9. Prominent garderobes on the thirteenth-century Chipchase Castle, Northumberland. (After Thompson 1975: pl. 114.)

In this light, ship-borne garderobes are best interpreted as external sanitary accommodations that were borrowed from castle architecture, entered from within, made of wood instead of stone, and projected from suitable "walls" of the vessels—in this case (see Fig. 2.4) the after face of the sterncastle. The overhang afforded direct deposition of excreta into the sea, much as the terrestrial garderobes permitted the deposit of their discharge into moats and pits. The shields on the counter of WA's *Kraeck* may well have been lead splash guards intended to inhibit the rotting of the counter.[27] Splash guards were not needed on castle walls because stone was much less susceptible to excreta-generated molds and fungi and of course were not subject to rot. The dark stains below the vents of most castle garderobes attest to the rich organic nature of the residues, though such accumulations on ships would have been lessened by wave action at the stern. Incidentally, taking a following sea while using these garderobes would have been quite an experience, especially if there was not a one-way flapper valve or something similar at the mouth or in the throat of the vent.

It has been suggested that ships' garderobes could have been used in a defensive capacity, "as a means of annoying boarders at the stern by pouring hot water or molten lead upon them," in addition to serving their primary function as "sanitary offices."[28] Garderobes were used throughout the fifteenth century and into the sixteenth, when they underwent important changes.

TURRETS/BARTIZANS. Another interesting feature apparent in depictions from the last quarter of the fifteenth century is the stern turret, square in plan, usually seen in pairs, and attached right aft on either side of the stern superstructure. In figure 2.10 are two vessels, probably Flemish, drawn by WA. They seem to be fishing craft, as evidenced by the horizontal barrels mounted outboard along the starboard bulwarks (Fig. 2.10B) and at the port quarter (Fig. 2.10A). An additional detail from the roughly contemporary painting entitled *The Rape of Helen*, by Gozzoli (Fig. 2.11), includes turrets in the same locations that are surmounted by crenelations, or battlements. Although all three pairs are quite similar, discernible differences in the turrets of these ships include crenelated tops, as opposed to pointed ones with or without knobs, and the absence of loops, or windows, in one pair. On the one turret that could provide evidence for the means of entry to these devices (Fig. 2.10B), no trace of any entrance is visible.

a

b

Fig. 2.10. Stern
turrets on two
vessels illustrated by
the master WA, late
fifteenth century.
(A) (After Nance
1913d: 67, fig. 1.)
(B) (After Nance
1911b: 66.)

Fig. 2.11.
Battlemented stern
turrets on a ship in
Gozzoli's The Rape
of Helen, late
fifteenth century.
(After Nance
1913d: 67, fig. 4.)

Moreover, the poorly detailed rendering of the undersides of the turrets of the Italian ship (Fig. 2.11) leaves a good deal to be desired. Yet despite the lack of such small but important clues, it is postulated that the stern turrets of this period represent yet another feature of medieval castle architecture that was directly adapted to shipboard purposes.

In medieval military architectural parlance, turrets that corbeled out at strategic points near entranceway arches or in the walls of towers, churches, and habitations were known as "bartizans."[29] Originally used in defensive and lookout capacities, they came to serve as sanitary accommodations. Occasionally, bartizan machicolations—defensive slots left between supports in their floors—were used as vents through which excreta was removed.[30] Figure 2.9 illustrates a type of round, corbeled, though unmachicolated, bartizan.

According to Thompson, bartizans were "common in French military architecture of the 13th and 14th centuries."[31] However, they were not as common in England during this or subsequent periods. Interestingly, turrets, or bartizans, were also rare on English ships and may have been used in French or French-influenced craft (e.g., Dutch-built French vessels) almost exclusively.[32]

Bartizans depicted on ships of the fifteenth century, with their ample overhang at the stern, most likely served as external hygienic accommodations in a fashion similar to that of the garderobes they closely resembled. In addition, they may have performed another function. Nance offers the following illumination: "of all WA's ships these two fisherboats alone have such turrets, which fact, taken with the necessity of lights to a fishing fleet, strongly tempts one to look upon them as lanterns" above and garderobes below.[33]

Fig. 2.12. Stern of a fifteenth-century carrack by Reuwich, in Breydenbach's Journey to Jerusalem, *1483. (After Howard 1979: 22, fig. 21.)*

SOIL-PIPES. A relatively small number of fifteenth-century depictions display what appears to have been some type of plumbing or venting, that is, soil-pipes, for sanitary accommodations in the sterns of larger vessels, such as carracks. In figure 2.12, a carrack with what might be soil-pipes is illustrated. The construction of this vessel is reminiscent of that of WA's *Kraeck*, with its "curved bare stanchions . . . and gallery right aft."[34] There were, apparently, no garderobes like those on the *Kraeck*, but the hen coop-like structure in the middle of the aft-projecting ledge and the somewhat enigmatic semicircular objects on either side of it seem to resemble the equipage on the sterns of southern carracks of the period (see Fig. 2.6).

Of importance here are the two small objects protruding from the underside of the projecting ledge. Their stark shadows hint that they were cylindrical and, therefore, are probably best explained as soil-pipes extending from the presumed circular hygienic devices above the ledge, with which they are clearly associated.

3

The Sixteenth Century

For the greater part of the sixteenth century, ships of moderate and large size were still regarded as "sea castles" that relied primarily upon offensive and defensive tactics and weaponry borrowed from land armies. Correspondingly, the garderobes and bartizans adopted from castle architecture and used aboard ships during the fifteenth century continued to be used, in slightly altered forms, for most of the following century. Steep-tubs, or "necessary tubs," were also employed throughout the sixteenth century, as were the simple disposal systems that included the scupperlike soil-pipes.

The Bow

Changes in the bow configurations of sixteenth-century ships had considerable impact on the development of more efficient external sanitary accommodations in this area. Further incorporation of the forecastle into the hull structure and framing occurred, while forecastle height was reduced. Of greatest importance to this study is the appearance and development of the "beakhead," or "head."

The beakhead first appeared during the reign of Henry VIII (1509–47), though precisely how the typical carrack forecastle of the fifteenth century became the beakhead of the sixteenth is not well understood. Generally, the "galley spur," actually a type of ram, appeared down low on the bows of carracks and other vessels early in the sixteenth century, and the length of the triangular forecastle's projecting apex was shortened. A little later, the galley spur was moved upward somewhat and elaborated while, by around 1550, the forecastle had been retracted to within the confines of the forward portion of the hull and fully incorporated into its fabric and framing.

The installation of the galley spur was an attempt to equip sailing ships with the oared galley's primary weapon, the ram, so that the two might meet on more equitable terms. It seems to have been readily accepted, because in the few years following its initial appearance it is evident in English, French, Spanish, and Portuguese depictions. The Spanish *Santa Ana* of 1525 clearly had the "very elaborate projection of the carrack forecastle" and the distinctive galley spur just a few feet above the waterline.[1] In figure 3.1, an English ship from the Anthony Roll (1546) displays these characteristic features.

The galley spur, when it first appeared, seems to have consisted of a relatively open framework that was occasionally topped with a figurehead of some kind. Later, in the 1540s, the spur was decked, probably first by the Spanish, to permit more effective handling of the "headgear" and the mounting of small guns in the bow, to help give the developing broadside ships the "end-on" firepower of galleys. Within a short time, rails were also added. Subsequently, a bulwark was "carried along each side of the structure, and the resulting [beak]head was in section a rectangular trough" (Fig. 3.2).[2]

By the last third of the century, there were some differences between the beakhead arrangements on Spanish, and probably Portu-

Fig. 3.1. Galley spur and projecting forecastle on the English Swallow, *from the Anthony Roll of 1546. (After Vaughan 1914: 38, fig. 4.)*

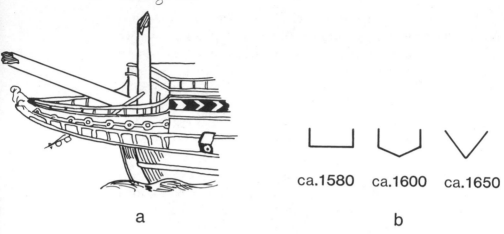

ca.1580　　ca.1600　　ca.1650

a　　　　　　　　　　　b

Fig. 3.2. Views of characteristic beakheads, ca. 1580–1650. (A) Late-sixteenth-century beakhead. (After Howard 1979: 106, fig. 146a.) (B) Cross-sectional views of characteristic beakheads, ca. 1580–1650. (After Howard 1979: 106, fig. 146b.)

guese, ships and those found on vessels that routinely plied more northern waters. On some Spanish vessels the area known as "the bows" was squared off athwartships and opened up at the lower level that would later be termed the gun deck, a level equal to that of the relatively low mounted beakhead. This made as many as three tiers of forward chase guns possible. In contrast, the beakheads of northern European ships were not placed as close to the water, probably owing to the rougher waters of the North Atlantic Ocean and North Sea. These beakheads were positioned at a height level with the main deck, upon which the forecastle stood.[3]

As the Spanish apparently developed the beakhead, so too were they the first to alter its form. By the last decade of the sixteenth century they were "steeving up" the knee of the head, or increasing the angle of the beakhead so as to shorten its forward projection and, consequently, decrease its area. The Spanish seem to have settled on an angle of about thirty degrees between the head and the waterline, although, once started, this trend toward shortening the projection of the head continued until well into the seventeenth century. Northern ships lagged behind in this regard; by around 1650, they had not yet exceeded the thirty-degree angle established by the Spanish more than fifty years earlier.[4]

In terms of hygiene, the beakhead was an improvement over the projecting forecastles of carracks. The heads were open to the natural cleansing actions of sun, wind, rain, and sea, whereas the forecastle projections had been more enclosed. Constructed as they were of relatively light framing, light planking, and gratings, beakheads were ideal platforms for the establishment of external sanitary accommodations. These probably consisted of rails or simple holed planks positioned as far away from the other activities performed there as possible, while still affording an unhindered drop to the sea. The whole would have been relatively easy to keep as clean as the common practices of the day prescribed.

It is important to note that, while the increased openness of the heads was a significant hygienic improvement over the closed forecastles of earlier vessels, the opposite is true of developments in the stern. There, the upperworks were becoming more enclosed to provide protection from the elements, which resulted in improved hygienic conditions. How these seemingly contradictory developments both contributed to the amelioration of sanitation on board can be easily explained by noting the uses to which each area was put: "There was indeed a great gulf fixed between the lower deck and the wardroom, a great disparity in victuals, in accommodation and in living conditions generally. Nowhere is this more marked than in the question, which must be considered fundamental, but which is much neglected by writers on the Service, of the ship's necessary arrangements."[5]

The forward area was the domain of the common seaman and consequently was much more crowded and given the least attention with respect to health and comfort. Therefore, construction that facilitated waste removal with little effort, maintenance, and expense was the norm. In contrast, the stern was the officers' area. Standing at the apex of the hierarchy, these men expected and were accorded accommodations better than those of common seamen. Comparatively, a much smaller number of men used the limited stern hygienic facilities, which were rigorously cleaned by the officers' underlings. Hence, the enclosed nature of the quarter galleries and their inherently more difficult maintenance were substantially less problematic.

One interesting description of the use of a sixteenth-century galley's sanitary accommodations has come to light. Generally, the configuration of the galley's bow would have been comparable to those of nonoared sailing ships of the period, so the following passage provides valuable insight: "It is a privilege of the galley that all passengers that want to evacuate the bowel and to produce something from their person are required to go to the latrines of the bow and lean against a head rail; and [in] what cannot be said, much less done, publicly without embarrassment, all of them are to be seen seated on the necessary as they have seen each other eating at the table."[6]

This account yields several clues about the use of the forward sanitary accommodations on Spanish galleys. Because the patrons of this particular facility perched on a "head rail," the head timbers of this galley's beakhead must have been fairly open and canted slightly outward, not vertical. Therefore, someone could have sat over a middle head rail and leaned back against the upper one. Apparently, these beakhead latrines could entertain a number of people simultaneously, the "embarrassment" of the situation aside.

To date, no archaeological evidence of beakhead structures or associated external sanitary accommodations has been recovered from sixteenth-century shipwrecks. Unfortunately, this is to be expected in the great majority of cases. Upper works of neither the bow nor the stern are likely to be preserved because they are usually the last elements to be covered by protective sediments. Consequently, they are exposed to the ravages of shipworms, tides, storms, and other destructive agents, such that we are left only with images in contemporary depictions and the sparse literary evidence.

The Stern

As forecastles had been integrated into the forward portions of hulls, the sterncastles of sixteenth-century ships also experienced further incorporation into the after hull structure. The placement of multiple counters at the stern and the extreme rake that resulted continued during the first half of the century. However, during the Elizabethan era, the number of overhangs, and therefore the rake, seem to have been somewhat reduced, at least in English vessels. The continental tendency was to retain the multiple counters.[7]

During the sixteenth century an important development related to the removal of human wastes was the appearance of stern and quarter galleries. Quarter galleries are of particular interest because it was in these stern structures that often elaborate external sanitary accommodations were to become firmly established and endure until the end of the nineteenth century.

STEEP-TUBS. Steep-tubs continued to be used throughout the sixteenth century, either for meat desalinization or as necessary tubs, both externally and within the hull. In their simplest forms, they were similar to the steep-tubs used during the preceding century and to modern Arab sanitary boxes. As such, they were slung over the upper bulwark or attached to the hull in order to provide a relatively unhindered drop to the sea and, at the same time, reasonable accessibility. Morison states that among Spanish seafarers "there was a good deal of joking" regarding the devices "hung over the rail forward and aft, for the seamen . . . to ease themselves." He adds that "they were called *jardines* [gardens], perhaps in memory of the usual location of the family privy."[8]

The external necessary tubs, according to depictions from this period, seem to have been moved from the sterns and quarters to the main chains of either or both sides of the hull sometime around midcentury. For vessels of most European nations, it is assumed that the tubs rested on the chain wale and were lashed to the hull or deadeyes. An excellent depiction of this arrangement on what was probably a Portuguese ship of circa 1562 is seen in figure 3.3. This change may have occurred because, among other things, the increased height

Fig. 3.3. Necessary tubs in port main chains. Detail of Armed Four-Master Putting to Sea, ca. 1562, by Frans Huys after Pieter Brueghel. (Reprinted by permission of the Rijksmuseum, Amsterdam.)

of sterncastles made necessary tubs on the quarters relatively inaccessible. For the same reason, steep-tubs used as meat softeners may well have retained their positions at the quarters, so that their remote locations inhibited pilfering by the crew.

There is an interesting reference to steep-tubs used as interior necessary tubs on English vessels in the last half of the sixteenth century. As in foregoing years, necessary tubs, into which the crew urinated, were placed at strategic points on the lower decks. There seem to have been standing orders in the British navy during this period to the effect that the necessary tubs were to be continuously "filled with urine and ready for use in the event of fire." It has been suggested that these orders imply a belief that urine had special firefighting qualities. However, this notion ignores the fact "that it was more reasonable to retain this liquid where it might put out a fire than to carry it to the upper deck, lower the bucket over the side, refill it with sea-water, and take it to a place where it could now no longer serve its primary purpose" because it was full.[9]

While no archaeological evidence for steep-tubs used as waste receptacles yet exists, there is some archaeological evidence of their employment in a meat-softening capacity. On the exterior of the preserved starboard section of the sterncastle of the *Mary Rose*, which foundered in 1545, a series of barrels were found just above the chain wale. Within them were a number of animal bones.[10]

GARDEROBES. The use of garderobes as external hygienic facilities in the sixteenth century is much less in evidence than for the previous century. In fact, there is a veritable dearth of both contemporary depictions and descriptions. Currently, only one illustration of garderobes is known from this period: a painting of approximately 1520, by an anonymous artist, entitled *The Embarkation of Henry VIII*. In it are shown some of Henry's largest vessels, among them what are popularly understood to have been the *Henry Grace à Dieu*, the *Great Bark*, and perhaps the *Mary Rose*. At the extreme after end of the starboard stern quarter of the *Great Bark*, a garderobe is clearly visible (Fig. 3.4). It is supported at a rakish angle by a pair of brackets underneath, between which is a vent in the floor. Presumably the stark, undecorated structure was sufficiently well aft and projected far enough outboard to allow a reasonably clean drop past the pronounced tumble home of the hull to the sea.

Even though fifteenth-century depictions of garderobes are any-

Fig. 3.4. Detail of The Embarkation of Henry VIII, ca. 1520, anonymous, showing a ship's quarter with garderobe attached. (Reproduced by gracious permission of Her Majesty Queen Elizabeth II.)

thing but abundant, there are enough to permit plausible conclusions to be drawn. In contrast, the striking sparseness of such representations from the sixteenth century is compelling. What happened to garderobes in the course of this hundred-year period?

Perhaps they fell victim to the general tendency of most European nations over the greater part of the century to build multiple counters at the stern. The number of overhangs and the rake of the sterncastle's after face might have made it prohibitively difficult to fit garderobes at the positions they had characteristically occupied on vessels of the previous century. However, the sides of the sterncastles above the tumble home were still generally vertical, flat surfaces upon which the garderobes could be installed easily, as in the case of the *Great Bark*. By assuming this configuration, garderobes may have been the true predecessors of enclosed quarter galleries, which made their first appearance early in the seventeenth century.

Another possible explanation for the disappearance of garderobes is that they were made somewhat redundant by the emergence of the "open balcony" style of stern and quarter galleries, which were employed as external sanitary accommodations.[11]

For the same reasons that beakheads, forecastles, and other superstructures are rarely preserved for archaeological examination, physical evidence for hygienic facilities in the sterns of sixteenth-century vessels is nonexistent. Perhaps as shipwrecks are found in deeper and more protective waters, the likelihood of finding preserved portions of upper works at both bow and stern and, consequently, associated external sanitary accommodations, will improve.

QUARTER GALLERIES. Quarter galleries provided an easily accessible, projecting platform on which to establish sanitary accommodations. First introduced in the 1530s, they took the form of an extension around the quarters of the unroofed stern galleries (Fig. 3.5).[12] But their acceptance and diffusion seem to have been rather slow, for they were uncommon as late as approximately 1555.[13] The first English depiction of a vessel with a quarter and stern gallery is that of the

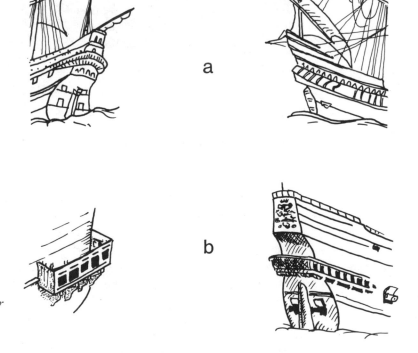

a

b

Fig. 3.5. Early styles of open quarter galleries, mid- to late sixteenth century. (A) Two ships by Le Testu. (After Howard 1979: 60, fig. 78.) (B) Two by Dutch artists. (After Laughton 1974: 162, figs. e, i.)

Greyhound, on the Anthony Roll of 1546.[14] When utilized, quarter galleries appear to have retained the open balcony configuration until the end of the century. Because the counters above stern galleries afforded some degree of protection from above, there was no need to cover them. The quarter galleries, however, were not protected by any such overhang, so to achieve some measure of protection, supports for awnings over them were erected.[15] The awnings were superseded by wooden coverings that increased the enclosure of the quarter galleries during the first third of the seventeenth century. These facilities originated as and remained the sole domain of the officers and important passengers throughout their long history. "Officers being officers, [quarter galleries were] handsomely built and decorated. . . ."[16]

The appearance of enclosed quarter galleries at the beginning of the seventeenth century may have resulted, in part, from the placement of garderobes on the quarters early in the sixteenth century. It seems logical that, after experiencing the relatively uncomfortable facilities consisting of open quarter and stern galleries, the need for more enclosure was loudly voiced, as partial coverings could not have offered the same degree of comfort as the "old style" garderobes. Moreover, shipwrights and finish carpenters were conservative: if something worked, they did not change it without compelling reasons. But if changes were to be made, why not reintroduce a device, albeit in an elaborated form, that had a proven record as an efficient and comparatively comfortable sanitary convenience?

TURRETS/BARTIZANS. It appears that turrets were not common in either British or continental navies or merchant fleets during most of the sixteenth century, or that they were not commonly depicted, or both. The only representations found were of a British naval vessel from the latter part of the century: the *Ark Royal,* flagship of the anti-Armada campaign of 1588. Although refitted several times, this ship originally had the characteristic beakhead, a single deck in the forecastle, and open stern and quarter galleries.[17] However, the surviving depictions present interpretational problems, as they might reflect the results of the numerous refits or be the products of artistic fancy.

Figure 3.6 comprises three depictions, all thought to represent the *Ark Royal.* Among them, almost every possible configuration of turrets and stern galleries is illustrated. One (Fig. 3.6A) displays high-

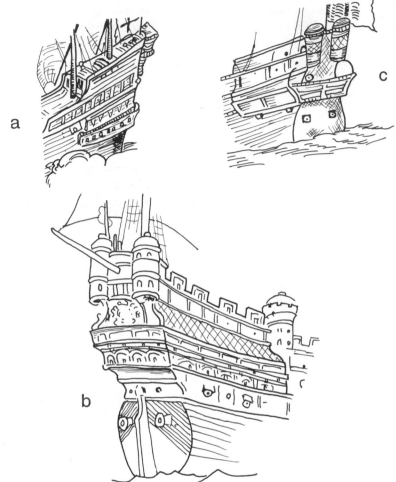

Fig. 3.6. Three depictions of the Ark Royal's *stern.*
(A) (After Nance 1914c: fig. 1.)
(B) (After Nance 1914c: fig. 3.)
(C) (After Nance 1914c: fig. 2.)

mounted stern turrets with an apparently open stern gallery. Another (Fig. 3.6B) shows high turrets (with a second pair just forward of the stern castle) and lacks a stern gallery, or has an enclosed gallery, while the third (Fig. 3.6C) evidences low-mounted stern turrets (or a low-ered superstructure) and open stern and quarter galleries. Of these, figure 3.6B suggests the most rational use of turrets as latrines. Ac-cording to the configurations in figures 3.6A and 3.6C, the effluent would not have had an unhindered drop to the sea, and its production would have been in full view of anyone on the open stern gallery, toward whom it probably would have been blown were they unfortunate enough to be there at the inopportune moment.

That the ship had stern turrets is certain, however. "What distinguished *Ark Royal* from her companion ships was the unusual construction of her after part. There were two turrets . . . at her stern and her poop bulwarks were battlemented. There may have been another pair of turrets at the forward end of the poop, used for latrines."[18] It is more reasonable to assume that, whether there were two pairs of turrets on the *Ark Royal* or only one, all of them conceivably could have been used as latrines, depending on the configuration of the stern gallery.

Evidently, turrets at the forward extremity of the poop were extremely rare throughout the age of sail, though depictions of some do exist, and they may have served a hygienic function in this location. Stern-mounted turrets, in contrast, were more common, and examples from the previous century are known. Yet problems arise when such structures mounted over open stern galleries are interpreted as having a hygienic function. If, indeed, the *Ark Royal* had open stern galleries in addition to stern turrets, then the latter must have been mounted high up on the stern to take advantage of the greater overhang. In this situation, the effluent from the turrets might have fallen relatively clear of the stern galleries. However, if the turrets were not mounted far enough aft, or perhaps when open galleries were mounted below, then special provisions, in the form of soil-pipes that carried the discharge down past the level of the stern galleries (see below), must have been made if the turrets served as sanitary facilities. If the turrets were mounted over a closed stern gallery or none at all, naturally there was no problem.

Alternatively, stern turrets might best be explained as poop lanterns, but even when mounted far enough aft, they could have served the dual purpose of lantern/latrine, as hypothesized for fifteenth-century turrets.

Although we have no other sixteenth-century turret depictions, there is one obscure reference to the *Elizabeth* of 1598 that offers additional evidence. The barbican on the side of the sterncastle is mentioned in a bill as having been painted.[19] The term "barbican" was generally applied to round defensive structures on medieval castles and, in this case, probably meant a turret mounted on or near the quarter.

The use and/or representation of turrets apparently experienced a resurgence at the end of the sixteenth century and throughout the seventeenth century, especially with regard to Danish, Dutch, and French vessels.

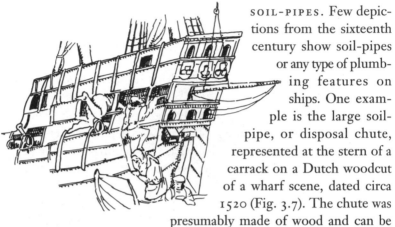

Fig. 3.7. Stern detail in the Ship of St. Stonybroke, *ca. 1520. (After de Groot and Vorstman 1980: 6, ill. 1.)*

SOIL-PIPES. Few depictions from the sixteenth century show soil-pipes or any type of plumbing features on ships. One example is the large soil-pipe, or disposal chute, represented at the stern of a carrack on a Dutch woodcut of a wharf scene, dated circa 1520 (Fig. 3.7). The chute was presumably made of wood and can be seen angling out of the stern just under the counter on the port side. Because the stern of this vessel was drawn with very little perceivable overhang, perhaps the chute served to direct the effluvia away from the stern more effectively. If there was a seat for this device, it was probably in a cabin on the halfdeck level and reserved for the use of the master or captain. "In Dutch vessels, and foreign [non-English] ships in general, latrines were inconspicuous, being arranged right aft, over the lower counter and entered from the great cabin. . . ."[20]

However, the chute may have facilitated the removal of other types of refuse; this might explain its rather large size in relation to the stern.

The Seventeenth Century

4

The seventeenth century was a period of dramatic change and innovation in external hygienic facilities: the beakhead was reduced in length and area, as its forward extremity was inclined more steeply (steeved up) from the waterline. Beakhead accommodations, for which the allotted area was consequently reduced, became individualized seats-of-ease toward the end of the century. The semicylindrical "roundhouse" was introduced at the juncture of the beakhead bulkhead and the main rail of the head. Latrine facilities appeared in the main chains, resting on the chain wale or on specially built shelves. Early in the century, quarter galleries were enclosed, were subsequently elaborated, and assumed prominent positions at the stern.

The seventeenth century is also characterized by the tendency to embellish with some type of florid design practically every external surface of a ship. From figurehead to stern gallery, no place remained undecorated, except the planking of the decks and the hull itself. Smooth, curving lines were embraced, while linear or angular features were scorned.

The Bow

The characteristic beakhead of the sixteenth-century galleon (see Fig. 3.2), projecting its exaggerated length approximately parallel to the waterline, slowly faded from favor during the first third of the seventeenth century. In its place, a sequence of transitional forms (Fig. 4.1) is evident for large- and moderate-sized naval and merchant vessels that, as noted above, followed in the wake of the trends set by the Spanish some fifty years earlier.

From about 1610 to 1640, the forward part of the beakhead was

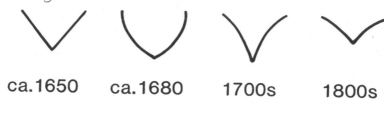

ca.1650   ca.1680   1700s   1800s

elevated farther from the water by means of a slight upward curve and tended to taper forward. During the 1640s, changes were more rapid. The steeving up of the knee of the head continued, while the head rails curved upward, taper increased, and solid sides were replaced with an open framework. The resulting structure was somewhat smaller and lighter, and the area reserved for activities there, including waste removal, was reduced. The figurehead became more and more upright as the angle of entry was increased to about thirty degrees.[1]

By around 1650, the basic form of the head, a shallow V in cross section and less "beaky" than before, had been effected and the pace of change had slowed.[2] Between 1650 and 1670, the shortening of the projection continued, thus decreasing further its area and probably reducing the number of locations that served a hygienic function. Greater upward curvature of the head rails was accompanied by the increasing verticality of the figurehead, until the inclination at the bow was some forty-five degrees.[3] Figure 4.2, a drawing of the head of the *Prince* of 1670, illustrates the form achieved by this time.

After about 1670, there were no fundamental changes in the configuration of the head, as only details were altered. The upper head rails were raised, which made the head deeper and afforded the installment of seats-of-ease at several levels. The head timbers became convex, thus creating a cross section that resembled something between a V and a U (Fig. 4.1). Sometime shortly after 1673, the round-house, a distinctive sanitary accommodation discussed below, made its appearance on either side of the beakhead bulkhead. Just prior to the end of the century, the head timbers straightened out again and then reversed curvature, becoming concave and fanning out above to meet the "main, or upper rails which in plan ran straight from the figures to the corners of the forecastle."[4] By 1700, a general scheme had been developed that endured until the end of the nineteenth century.

Fig. 4.2. Head of the Prince, *1670. (After Howard 1979: 106, fig. 146c.)*

Meager archaeological evidence for beakhead conveniences exists in the form of one piece of lead plumbing, which is purported to be a "pissdale" pipe. Pissdales were simple troughlike urinals placed at various locations forward and amidships, usually on the upper decks. A flanged lead pipe, which was probably part of one of these devices, was located on the wreck of the *Dartmouth*, sunk in 1690.[5] Because of its association with assorted items of hardware representative of bow sections of vessels, the pipe is assumed to have been part of the bow accommodations.[6] Serving a pissdale at the bow, the pipe would have extended almost vertically from the base of the urinal trough through the gratings and head beams.

SEATS-OF-EASE. Sometime between 1670 and 1680, distinct individual sanitary facilities, or seats-of-ease, placed within the structure of the head and equipped with "trunking," or drainage sluices, to direct the discharge downward, made their first appearance on models (Fig. 4.3).[7] It is assumed that they were introduced on real ships at the same time, though they may very well have been used earlier on European vessels.

Without exception, depictions dated to the earlier years of the seventeenth century seem to have been drawn at angles that prohibit discernment of any details regarding the construction or placement of accommodations in the head. Fortunately, we have actual archaeological evidence from 1628, in the bow of the Swedish warship *Wasa*

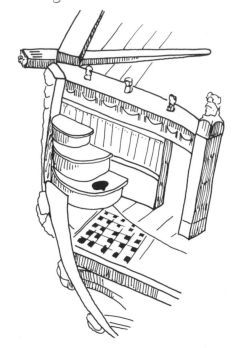

Fig. 4.3. Hole only in lower level, on a model of the English forty-six-gun ship Mordaunt (1681); the upper two levels were probably steps to the deck over the forecastle. Another hole and gratings are to port. (After Munday 1978: 135, fig. 1.)

(Figs. 4.4–4.6).[8] A single seat of ease is located on each side of the beakhead against the aft face of a beakhead frame, approximately three meters forward of the stem. In this position, there was clear access to the sea below. The accommodations consisted of simple rectangular boxes that projected about one-half meter above the beakhead floor, such that the inner head rails made good back rests. Atop the starboard box is a wood fragment that seems to be a remnant of a "seat" that received the anatomy of the users, who faced inboard. When they did appear on models later in the century, seats-of-ease were placed "over the bow on the gratings of the beakhead," originally situated "in the angle between the top [head] rail and the beakhead bulkhead, on each side" (Fig. 4.3).[9]

Having an unhindered drop to the sea, these areas were also the most protected, relatively speaking, in the open works of the beakheads "but would hardly encourage loiterers in anything but calm weather, besides which there must have been constant pressure from men awaiting their turn. The advantage of having spray, not to say seas breaking over the head when the vessel was under sail, or in a rough anchorage, and so cleansing the area, must at the same time have rendered it uncomfortable and even dangerous from the seaman's point of view."[10]

Despite the bathing action of the waves, the task of washing the beakhead may have proved uncomfortable for the seamen. Apparently, the drop to the sea was not always a completely clear one. John Smith states that punishment for lying was having to "keep clean the beakhead, and chains" beneath.[11]

A wide variety of configurations were employed: seats were placed on one, two, and three levels; on either side of the bowsprit; or at

Fig. 4.4. Seat-of-ease (right foreground) on the starboard side of the Wasa's beakhead, looking forward, 1628. (Photo by G. Ilonen. Reprinted by permission of the VasaMuseet, Stockholm.)

lower levels athwart the head. The bow accommodations on a model of an English ship of forty-six guns (Fig. 4.3) consist of a set of three tiers, of which only the bottom one is pierced, on either side of the beakhead bulkhead. "This is not provided with a round hole, but with an aperture of a far more tailored shape. . . ."[12] This "tailored shape" is that of a keyhole and is known from Roman latrines of stone and wood, as well as from the Bremen cog of circa 1380 (see Fig. 2.2).[13]

Fig. 4.5. The
Wasa's port seat-
of-ease in the
beakhead, looking
forward. (Photo by
G. Ilonen.
Reprinted by
permission of the
VasaMuseet,
Stockholm.)

Fig. 4.6. The
Wasa's starboard
seat-of-ease as it
would have been
used. (Photo by
G. Ilonen. Reprinted
by permission of the
VasaMuseet,
Stockholm.)

Gratings were used as before, and as they would continue to be.

Figure 4.7 illustrates another configuration on a model from 1692 of a larger, eighty-gun English ship, the *Boyne*. Here a single, keyhole seat is seen at the juncture of the top rail and the beakhead bulkhead. Gratings occupy most of the area of the head platform and an isolated seat is mounted on the gratings on the starboard side of the bowsprit. On these isolated seats-of-ease, the keyhole slot, when evident in representations, indicates which direction the user would have faced; in this instance, it was outboard. This model exhibits facilities only on the starboard side of the head—a mere two accommodating appliances for a large portion of the approximately 650-man crew of an eighty-gun ship!

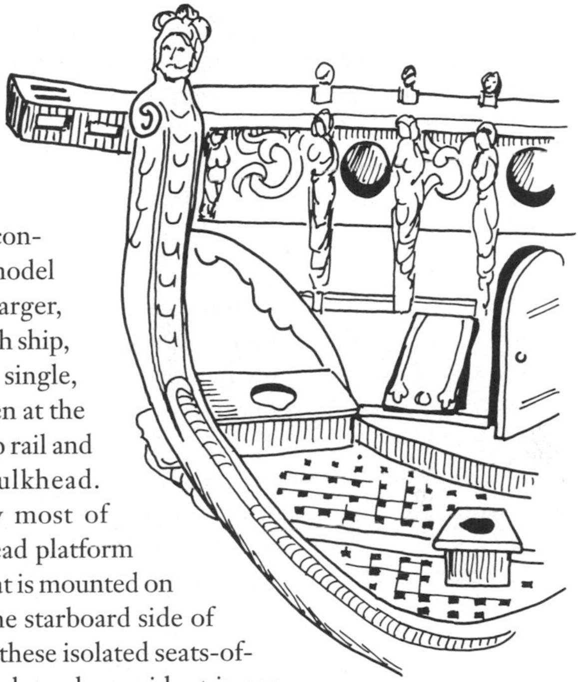

Fig. 4.7. Starboard seating only, on a model of the English eighty-gun ship Boyne, *1692. (After Munday 1978: 135, fig. 4.)*

Trunking was fitted to the individual seats-of-ease. Usually square in section, these wooden chutes projected down through the head timbers and terminated just below the knee of the head. Figure 4.8 shows one of these seats in use, with the sailor facing outboard and the trunking, labeled *14*, running through the head timbers.

FORE TURRETS AND ROUNDHOUSES. A peculiar feature seen in a handful of depictions of seventeenth-century French vessels is the

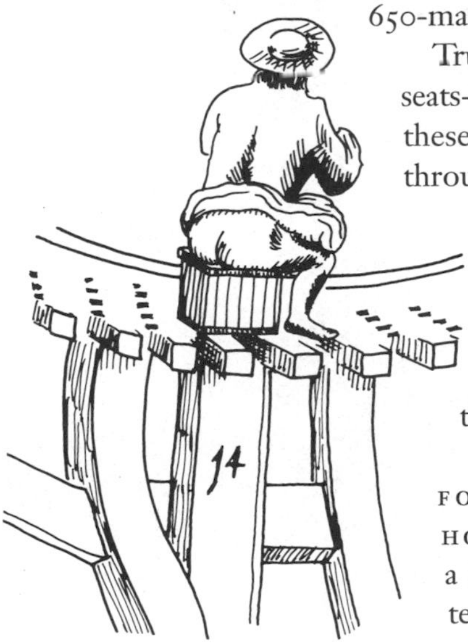

Fig. 4.8. A freestanding seat-of-ease with square trunking (labeled 14), user facing outboard. (After Munday 1978: 133, tailpiece.)

fore turret. It first appears in an etching of the *Navire Royale* of 1626
(Fig. 4.9) and another Dutch-built French ship, located just abaft the
beakhead to port; presumably there was one to starboard as well.[14]
The only other depictions of fore turrets found were in that of *La
Couronne*, built in 1638, and they were located in the same positions
as those of the other two French ships.[15] Thus, projecting out from
the ship's sides at a level that might have allowed interior access from
within the forecastle, fore turrets were potential locations for sanitary
facilities. However, what seems to have been a rather short period of
use hints at inherent problems. It appears that they were light structures attached to a part of the hull that was buffeted by waves in any
but following seas. As a result, fore turrets would have been vulnerable and subject to loss.

Laughton knows of no other ships that were depicted as having
fore turrets. He adds that the fore turret seems "to have been peculiar
to the French, and there is little doubt that [it was] the ancestor of the
later round house in the head, which [is] found in French ships about
1690."[16]

Fig. 4.9. Detail of the Navire Royale, *1626, anonymous (Hondius?). (Reprinted by permission of the Rijksmuseum, Amsterdam.)*

Navire Royale
faicte en Hollande
Anno 1626

Roundhouses, or semicylindrical hygienic accommodations placed at either side of the beakhead bulkhead, are generally thought to have been introduced by the English at the beginning of the eighteenth century; at least the first representations of them are on English ship models dated to 1703.[17] On one (Fig. 4.10A), a single roundhouse is located on the starboard side of the head; it has been proposed that this may be indicative of a transitional stage that preceded the standard configuration of a pair of roundhouses.[18] Another model of the same date is fitted with a pair of roundhouses (Fig. 4.10B), which seems to suggest that the transition was very rapid. But in view of the generally slow rate of change in other features of ships, this would seem unlikely; perhaps this one example of a single roundhouse is simply an aberration.

If the single roundhouse on the model of 1703 does not evince a transitional period, then there must have been earlier occurrences. Could the French fore turrets and the reported appearance of roundhouses on French ships of around 1690 be the forerunners of roundhouses on English vessels? This is certainly possible, but the latter might also have resulted in part from a slow development initiated by the English as early as 1668.

In that year, following the disastrous defeat of the English at the

Fig. 4.10. Views of roundhouses on two ships, 1703. (A) Starboard roundhouse only, with round seats to port and starboard, on a 1703 model of an English ninety-six-gun ship. (After Munday 1978: 136, fig. 7.) (B) Detail of roundhouse with soil-pipe on another 1703 model of a first-rate. (After Munday 1978: 136, fig. 6.)

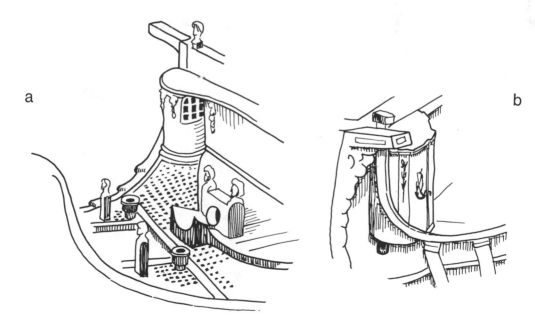

a

b

Battle of the Medway in 1667, the ninety-six-gun *Charles* (later the *Royal Charles* and *St. George*) was built. "She was the first of the 'great ships' to appear after the [second Anglo-Dutch] war" and was extremely popular.[19] Of interest to this study is the fact that in the middle of the deep two-level beakhead bulkhead the ship was fitted with a set of three semicircular, ballustraded galleries that projected forward from the upper deck level (Fig. 4.11). At first glance, roundhouses do seem to be present; a closer look reveals the lifted lid of a port in the beakhead bulkhead beneath what is actually the starboard gallery. Obviously, the space below was left open.[20]

If the spaces underneath the outer two galleries were simply closed in with screening or light planking and incorporated the seats at each after corner of the head, or if a hole pierced the head platform in the resulting compartment, then a serviceable sanitary facility would have been created.[21] Moreover, the area on each side of the beakhead bulkhead had become relatively unused because chase guns had been forced from the forecastle by the increased height of the head. This location was therefore a "natural" spot upon which to erect latrines, as the overhang was sufficient to allow a free drop to the sea. There would have been easy access to these facilities through the forecastle and, as enclosed and much more comfortable hygienic accommodations, their use would have been a privilege coveted by petty officers, midshipmen, mates, and others whose status was above that of the common seaman.

In light of the popularity of the *Charles*, the tendency of ship-

Fig. 4.11. Details of the bow of the ninety-six-gun ship Charles, *1668. Note the three semicircular galleries on the beakhead bulkhead. (After Fox 1980: 95, fig. 104.)*

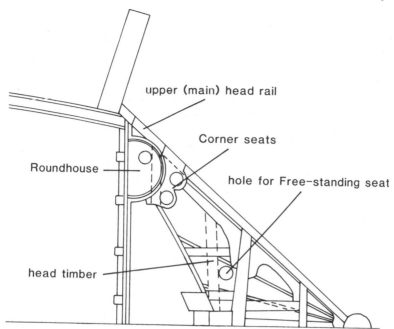

upper (main) head rail

Corner seats

Roundhouse

hole for Free-standing seat

head timber

Fig. 4.12. Plan of the head of the English Suffolk, 1765. (After Lavery 1984: 141, fig. 2.)

wrights to imitate the styles of trendsetting designs on popular vessels, and the fact that there are references in the Admiralty surveys of 1674–80 that suggest the presence of roundhouses, it would seem that their development could have stemmed from the fusion of the French fore turret and a structure that serendipitously resulted from the imitation of a particular style of embellishment—the semicircular head gallery like those of the *Charles*.[22] Figure 4.12 is a schematic diagram of the general layout of roundhouses and seats-of-ease of the eighteenth century, but it serves to illustrate the configuration of roundhouses that became more or less standard by the end of the seventeenth century (cf. Fig. 4.10).

Amidships

In larger ships, auxiliary hygienic conveniences were added at locations amidships. Pissdales were not only placed in the head but were also installed against the bulwarks on upper decks, and presumably middle decks as well. A pissdale located forward on the upper deck just abaft the forecastle bulkhead is seen in a depiction of a first-rate of around 1680.[23] A model from the first years of the eighteenth century exhibits one in roughly the same position (Fig. 4.13).

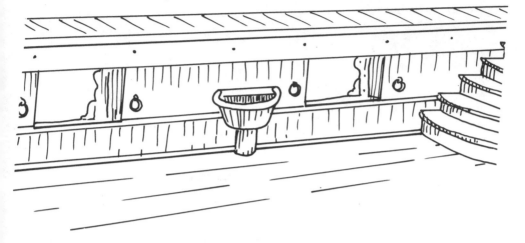

Fig. 4.13. Pissdale on the port side, forward, on a 1703 model of an unidentified English ship of ninety guns. (After Munday 1978: 136, fig. 8.)

SIDE-SHELVES. During the early seventeenth century, a type of sanitary accommodation carried roughly amidships, in or near the main chains, first appeared primarily in depictions of English vessels. In a painting by A. Willaert (ca. 1613), an English ship displays a side-shelf, as they are called, mounted on a support bracket located below the starboard main chains (Fig. 4.14).

In this instance, the side-shelf was a "solid square structure, roofed in and railed about at its top." Nance adds that, because no external entrance is apparent, the side-shelf must have been "a built-out latrine entered from within."[24] Just forward of the side-shelf, on the same support bracket, are three steep-tubs. The latter certainly would have served in their food preparation role, for the appearance of the side-shelf must have made them redundant as sanitary facilities.

It should be remembered that, during the sixteenth century, steep-tubs that are thought to have performed a waste-disposal role were located in the main chains (see Fig. 3.3) and, over roughly the same period, garderobes were moved from the stern transom to a position on the stern quarter. In the late sixteenth and very early seventeenth centuries, garderobes moved to the fore end of the quarter galleries.[25] With another short move forward into the main chains, the early, angular side-shelf would have been born. In addition, the Willaert representation seems to constitute evidence that "there was a period during which, rather than cumber the chains with steep-tubs and latrines together, English seamen carried both latrines and steep-tubs on a specially-built separate shelf below."[26]

Moreover, side-shelves appear to have been located on the starboard side, opposite the larboard-side entry port, when there was one. In fact, "it seems to have been an invariable rule" and may be an explanation for the use of the term "port" as an alternative for larboard.[27] It is notable that a disproportionate number of depictions were found in which the port sides of vessels are illustrated.

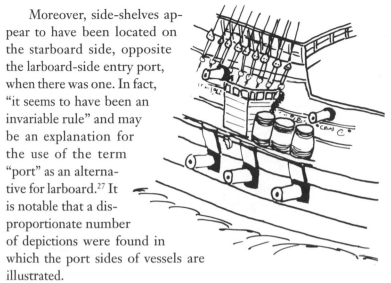

Fig. 4.14. Early starboard side-shelf on separate ledge with three steep-tubs. (After a painting by A. Willaert, ca. 1613, in the Scheepvaart Museum, Amsterdam.)

In the last half of the seventeenth century, side-shelves, when fitted, evidently assumed a semicylindrical shape, possibly as a result of the rather antiangular influences of the baroque style. The introduction of a second entry port on the starboard side of most two- and three-deckers, beginning about 1670, may have displaced the side-shelves or hastened their retirement from common use by about 1700.[28] Perhaps they were employed thereafter primarily as temporary accommodations, erected only when needed.

The Stern

The baroque fashions popular during the seventeenth century were most apparent on the sterns of ships. Generally, the larger or more important the vessel, the more elaborate were the decorations. The *Sovereign of the Seas* (1637) is considered by many to have been the finest English example of baroque-style embellishment and grace. With regard to hull forms, the heights of the sterncastles were reduced, stern and quarter galleries at two and occasionally three levels appeared, and quarter galleries were largely enclosed. The extensive elaboration of the quarter galleries made them the most prominent features at the stern.

Another change in the appearance of ships' sterns was spurred by the adoption—actually reintroduction—of the round-shaped hull, or "round tuck." The English seem to have initiated this development in the first half of the century in an effort to improve sailing capabilities.

Most continental navies and merchant fleets followed suit over the succeeding fifty years, but the Spanish and Dutch resisted this change until shortly after approximately 1725.[29] The shape of the hull below the sterncastle was of little consequence, as the round-tuck stern had little effect on the hygienic functionality of quarter galleries.

GARDEROBES. Garderobes were depicted only at the forward ends of ships' quarter galleries in the first two decades of the seventeenth century. They are seen isolated on quarter galleries that are open (Fig. 4.15) or partly enclosed; no representations of garderobes associated with completely enclosed quarter galleries were found. So in an apparently transitional stage in the development of either enclosed quarter galleries or side-shelves or both, garderobes played one last role before becoming virtually nonexistent in subsequent depictions.

QUARTER GALLERIES AND TURRETS. The first third of the seventeenth century witnessed the increasing enclosure of the quarter galleries, a process that may have received some impetus from the

Fig. 4.15. Garderobe isolated at forward end of quarter gallery, early seventeenth century. (After Laughton 1974: 162, fig. b.)

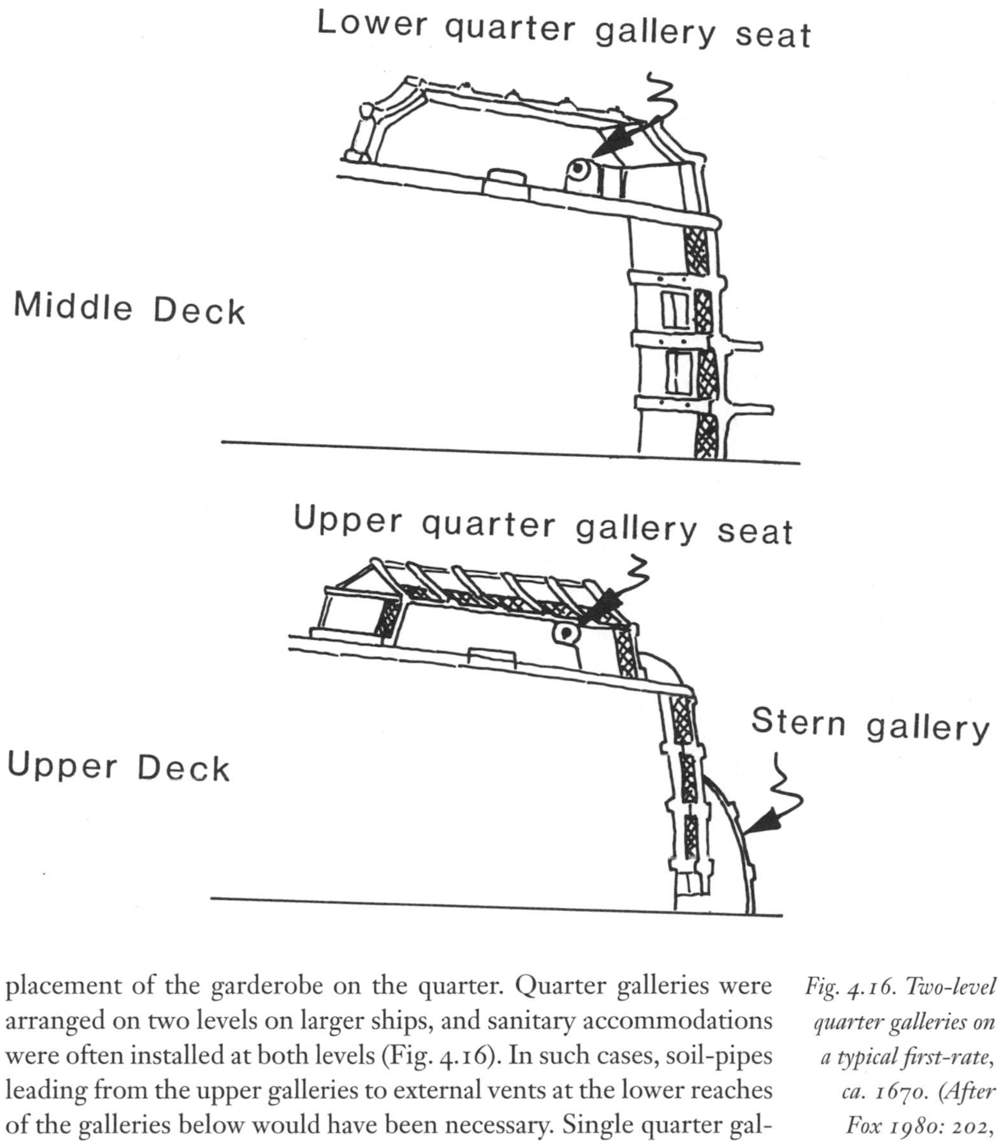

Lower quarter gallery seat

Middle Deck

Upper quarter gallery seat

Stern gallery

Upper Deck

placement of the garderobe on the quarter. Quarter galleries were arranged on two levels on larger ships, and sanitary accommodations were often installed at both levels (Fig. 4.16). In such cases, soil-pipes leading from the upper galleries to external vents at the lower reaches of the galleries below would have been necessary. Single quarter galleries, or those at the lowest level, customarily were fitted with a short length of soil-pipe leading directly down from the latrine, through the lower finishing of the structure. Oddly, the quarter galleries on the *Wasa* (1628) were not pierced for this purpose.[30] If they saw service as the officers' toilets, perhaps chamber pots or the like were used.

The function of quarter galleries did not change, but it is evident

Fig. 4.16. Two-level quarter galleries on a typical first-rate, ca. 1670. (After Fox 1980: 202, plans H, I.)

that their appearance was altered a great deal during the seventeenth century. These transformations are beyond the scope of this book, but it should be noted that the stern turrets of the later years of the sixteenth century and those that appeared on English, Danish, and French vessels (see Fig. 4.9) in the next century were incorporated into the design and structure of the quarter galleries. Thus the hygienic function of turrets was combined with that of quarter galleries.

The grand-scale elaboration of the seventeenth century yielded to a relatively stark, generally utilitarian appearance in the course of the eighteenth and nineteenth centuries, but hygienic accommodations remained virtually unchanged.[1] Only minor alterations were made in the number and configuration of facilities in the heads of large vessels. A pair of roundhouses and from two to six freestanding seats-of-ease continued to be used throughout the period. Quarter galleries with one, two, and occasionally three levels remained the principal conveniences for senior officers, while pissdales amidships were auxiliary features heavily relied upon by the crew.

Side-shelves, however, were not depicted in this period. It should be remembered that, during the last third of the seventeenth century, side-shelves on large vessels were probably displaced by second entry ports installed on the starboard side in or near the area previously assigned to such accommodations. An appreciation of their vulnerable position, in addition to changes made during the eighteenth century regarding the location of fore and main channels, may have jointly contributed to the further displacement and modification of side-shelves.[2]

The Bow

SEATS-OF-EASE. The eighteenth and nineteenth centuries witnessed a tendency to increase the flair of the head, as seen in cross section (see Fig. 4.1). This created greater surface area upon which to install more gratings, increased the number of freestanding necessary seats, and permitted the arrangement of grouped, multihole conveniences placed against the forward-most part of the bows.[3]

In the detailed construction plans available from this two hundred–year period, there is a serious lack of diagrams of the hygienic facilities at the head. Munday's assertion that their design and placement were apparently left to the "imagination or whim of the shipbuilder" might be refined with the idea that shipwrights had no need of such details in plans.[4] They knew how best to fit the facilities of the day to the vessels they built. In any case, the best source of information on bow accommodations for this period is the large number of contemporary models, which attest to a great variety of configurations.

Freestanding seats-of-ease were installed, singly or in pairs, on the gratings at either side of the bowsprit, next to the gammonings.[5] They were usually square and mounted on square trunking (Fig. 5.1); a small number of round seats with either round or square trunking are known. One disgruntled passenger of the mid-eighteenth century described the trunking in less than respectful terms: "Those more vulgar tubes that downward peep, near where the Lion awes the raging deep . . ."[6] If the trunking did not extend to the waterline in some manner, then it was "poised over the sea [such that] it would have been incautious for a party of ladies and gentlemen to hire a boat for amusement and pull around among the anchored ships, say in Portsmouth Harbor or Spithead. . . . To pause on such an aquatic excursion to admire the gilded figurehead would be an error which was doubt-

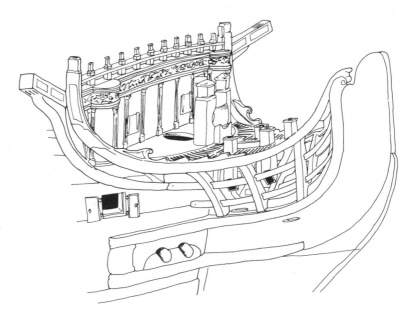

Fig. 5.1. Bow accommodations on a model of the English Princess Royal, *a second-rate of 1773. Note the two roundhouses and four freestanding seats with square trunking. (After Stevens 1949: 75.)*

less well enough known to the local boatmen. By the same token, it would be imprudent to loiter under the quarter, even if the carved work was of extraordinary quality."[7]

Some double, triple, and quadruple seats were located at lower levels within the head, usually arranged athwartships. Using these particular conveniences must have been a "wet ride rivalling a fairground Big Dipper, as the ship pitch[ed] into a sea."[8]

Examples of typical hygienic facilities in the heads of large vessels of circa 1800 are provided by Nelson's *Victory*. This ship was equipped with two pairs of freestanding seats-of-ease and one tucked in each corner by the roundhouses. This was a total of only six formal sanitary accommodations forward for the roughly eight hundred–man complement of this first-rate.[9]

In 1811 the beakhead bulkhead was officially abolished and the "round bows" were introduced. This was deemed necessary because of the vulnerability of the bulkhead to head-on enemy fire. Unable to withstand onslaughts from carronades and other ship-smashing guns, the beakhead bulkhead had left the upper deck relatively unprotected.[10] The appearance of the round bow did not affect the function of the head or seriously alter its shape, but it did precipitate modifications in the design and placement of crew facilities. More multihole appliances were used. Settles, or drainage catchments, pissdales, and simple holed seats were incorporated into a variety of configurations, usually placed on either side of the stem outboard of the forward-most part of the hull (Fig. 5.2).

Around 1811, the trunking, or soil-pipes, became less conspicuous, especially if they were single soil-pipes from multihole units placed close to the bows. In this location, trunking led directly down to the waterline against the hull planking or was nestled in the angle formed by the stem and planking. Soil-pipes were often disguised by being painted in the accepted fashions and colors of the day (Fig. 5.2) or were incorporated into the hawse bolsters and cheek pieces. The inclusion of roundhouse soil-pipes in cheek pieces began in the middle of the eighteenth century. Two models (ca. 1750) in the Museo Naval in Madrid display such soil-pipes: one is of the *Rayo*, a Spanish vessel lost in the Bay of Cadiz after the Battle of Trafalgar, and the other is of an unidentified *navio*. On a model of a Dutch first-rate of around 1800 in the Scheepvaart Museum, Amsterdam, a soil-pipe descends from a three-hole settle through the cheek pieces to the waterline.

Sometime around the middle of the nineteenth century, exten-

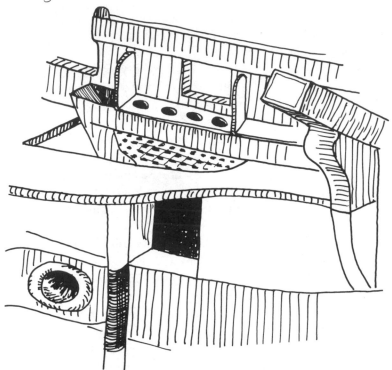

Fig. 5.2. Four-hole settle with pissdale on a model of the eighty-gun ship Collingwood, *1841; soil-pipe extends to the waterline. (After Munday 1978: 140, fig. 24.)*

sive changes in bow designs were brought about by the emergence of iron-hulled ships and were no doubt spurred by the advent of steam propulsion. The increased velocity of steamships necessitated a sharper bow configuration to facilitate slicing through the waves rather than riding over or battering through them, as most sailing vessels were prone to do. Areas at the bow that had effectively served hygienic functions in sailing ships were increasingly claimed by ground tackle, steam winches, and other equipment required for routine ship-handling tasks. Thus only the term "head" remained in use, as a euphemism for any ship's hygienic facilities. "The disuse of this great convenience, having the seats-of-ease poised over the sea, must have been gradual. Clearly the structure of the ship was changing, the advent of iron in shipbuilding heralded new designs and the removal of the heads amidships, so to say."[11]

The issue of relative wind direction probably had little influence on the removal of hygienic facilities from the bows of steam-powered (as opposed to sail-powered) vessels. The blow-back of effluvia from the bow onto the hull, resulting from the ability of steamships to head directly into the wind, a feat sailing ships were unable to accomplish, was certainly an insignificant factor compared to the relatively increased scouring and cleansing action of the sea at the bows of such ships.

Generally, steamships can serve as yet another illustration of the main tenet of this work: that waste-disposal accommodations were customarily erected on appropriate outboard projections of ships in all periods. The overhanging construction features of steamships' paddle boxes, whether of side- or sternwheelers, offered exceptional opportunities to erect effective hygienic facilities. Further, the agitated water in the vicinity of the paddle wheels ensured the efficient dissolution and dispersal of the effluvia.

To return to sailing ships, the accommodations amidships were still inadequate for the number of men carried aboard ships in this period. An account from about 1870 describes conditions on a general depot ship, HMS *Duke of Wellington*, stationed at Portsmouth. This ship was equipped with simple six-hole platforms on each side; no partitions were provided. From "four A.M. until long after pipedown at night there were queues of waiting men on each side of the upper deck struggling to reach the heads." It appears that often only the strongest were successful. "There were numbers of men daily who were in the report for offences against decency. While every morning care had to be taken to remove the evidence of such offences in scores of places. . . ."[12]

ROUNDHOUSES. Roundhouses continued to be employed throughout the eighteenth and nineteenth centuries in basically the same form as that developed in the course of the preceding century, as seen clearly on a number of models housed in European museums. In addition to the many examples of roundhouses on models supplied by Munday, the National Maritime Museum in Greenwich has two models, one of an unidentified sixty-gun English ship of circa 1720 and another of an unidentified fifty-gun vessel of circa 1725. Each has a pair of roundhouses in conjunction with corner seats. The Museo Naval exhibits at least five models from the mid- to late eighteenth century that display this standard configuration. The model of the *Real Carlos* of 1766 has single corner seats, while that of the *San Justo* (1779–1826) is fitted with corner seats-of-ease in two tiers, the upper seats of which are each equipped with a back. The mouths of the lead-lined soil-pipes from these grouped conveniences are evident on the underside of the head platform.

About 1732, slightly modified roundhouses were installed in the bows of sloops of war and small frigates when these types of vessels were built with round bows.[13] After the abolishment of the beakhead bulkhead in 1811, roundhouses were simply moved into the forward part of the forecastle and retained their relative positions in the ship. Still installed in pairs at this time, the port roundhouse was for the use of mates, midshipmen, and warrant officers, while the starboard facility served the sick bay with which it was customarily associated.[14] Sick bays had been placed on the starboard side, in or under the forecastle, starting about 1800.

Amidships

The use of pissdales at various locations amidships continued unabated throughout the period. They were often installed forward and aft against the bulwarks in the waists on contemporary models (see Fig. 4.13). At least six other examples of pissdales on unidentified models in the collection of the National Maritime Museum, Greenwich, are known to exist. Two of these, one of a fifty-gun ship of circa 1720 and another of the same size from circa 1725, have paired pissdales, one on each side of the forward jeer capstans. A model of an unidentified one hundred–gun first-rate of around 1725 exhibits a pissdale in the waist that takes the form of a rimmed basin set on the deck and not installed against the bulwark, as was the common practice.

In contrast, no depictions are known of side-shelves on ships of the eighteenth or nineteenth centuries. Were side-shelves not used after the seventeenth century? Perhaps, but it seems more likely that they simply assumed a temporary function, being used only when needed, or they may have resurfaced in the late nineteenth century in the form of the six-hole platforms placed port and starboard amidships, mentioned above. As relatively light structures whose foundations, the fore and main channels, were always in place, side-shelves could have been jury-rigged easily. Moreover, if side-shelves were still mounted predominantly on the starboard side, they might not appear in the pictorial record due to the frustratingly persistent tendency of contemporary artists to depict the port sides of ships.

The Stern

Quarter galleries also continued to serve their same functions in the same manner throughout most of this two hundred–year period. Models of the first-rate *San Juan Nepomuceno* (1766–1805) and the

San Justo (1779–1826) in the Museo Naval evince two-level quarter galleries. The lower levels of the latter have single benches pierced with two holes. The model of a Dutch first-rate of around 1800 also has dual-level quarter galleries that are separately plumbed. The mouths of the soil-pipes are located on the after faces of the lower finishings of the quarter, as was standard.

Of course, some slightly modified forms of quarter gallery facilities were used by the European navies. The pierced bench seats often employed by the British and most continental navies and merchant fleets seem not to have been used on French ships of the late eighteenth century. The accommodations consisted of simple holes over which one squatted, with earthenware "footprints" on either side of the hole (cf. Fig. 2.8).[15]

A description of similar sanitary conveniences on an American vessel of 1793 was given, curiously enough, by a Frenchman: "In such a well appointed cabin, it is something of a shock to find that needs which might offend the nostrils must be satisfied through a hole in the floor, near the starboard windows. Cleanliness condemns this practice, and its practicability is so doubtful as to make one prefer a bottle."[16]

Apparently, early flushing water closets were first installed in the quarter galleries of British ships of the line in 1779.[17] However, they do not appear to have been used extensively until well into the 1800s. Toward the end of the nineteenth century, quarter galleries were eliminated when the "wide overhung stern of convention had been abandoned in favour of an oval underhung stern devoid of quarter galleries and ornamentation. . . . This type of stern lightened the ship aft, and improved on the older kinds in every way, except that it greatly reduced the accommodation for officers."[18] The era of internal, plumbed sanitary conveniences had begun.

A classic anecdote about the lively nature of life at sea, in spite of the often abominable conditions, revolves around a particular activity that occurred in the quarter gallery of a certain ship. It evokes an illuminating final image:

> *Stories . . . have been handed down and one such, its ingredients undeniably basic, concerns a seaman on board a sailing passenger vessel who, during a long voyage, was one day over the side, painting the ship's hull. His work took him to the vicinity of the quarter gallery and he became aware not only that it was occupied, but also that the occupant was female. Whatever urge it was that made him dab upwards with his brush,*

indeed whether he thought to claim it as an accident, cannot be known, but the result was an outraged passenger's complaint to the captain. The indiscipline was, of course, punished and the offence logged. The wording of the entry in the ship's log, was the cause of no small cogitation, but the final version was in its way a masterpiece: ". . . that he did paint an uncaulked seam."[19]

Conclusion 6

The foregoing is an examination and analysis of the development of shipboard external hygienic accommodations that were made possible by the construction of platforms at bow and stern. Later known as forecastles and sterncastles, such platforms consisted of overhangs and projections on which facilities that emptied directly into the sea were erected. Projecting shelves and chain wales on ships' sides provided other structures upon which accommodations were fitted.

The development of external sanitary conveniences was born of attempts to improve the normally horrendous hygienic conditions on ships of the fifteenth through nineteenth centuries. As vessels began to be decked over to improve their seaworthiness, and to offer greater protection from the elements and relatively more comfort, a number of factors combined to lessen, even negate, such positive effects. The consequent decrease in ventilation and light in the spaces below and between decks was a serious matter. Of overriding importance was that placing living surfaces (decks) one above another created a bird-cage-like environment, in which every imaginable bit of debris, filth, and human effluvia gravitated from upper to lower levels.

The study of contemporary depictions of ships and descriptions of life at sea combined with historical analyses of ship construction, shipboard life, and naval medicine have yielded a history of the use of external sanitary accommodations for the period in question. Figure 6.1 is a flow diagram that graphically summarizes the developments of, and relationships among, these facilities through time.

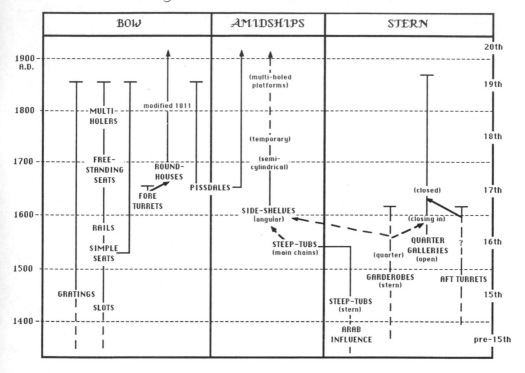

BOW	AMIDSHIPS	STERN

Fig. 6.1. Time line and flow diagram of the development of external sanitary accommodations.

The Bow

Evidence of hygienic conveniences in the projecting bow structures (beakheads, or heads) of ships of the fifteenth and sixteenth centuries is admittedly sketchy. Inferences as to their nature, based on simple logic, have been drawn from more detailed data from the seventeenth century. Wooden gratings, slots in the flooring, rails of the beakhead, and simple, holed boards as seats have all been suggested as having served a hygienic, waste-disposal function during the fifteenth and sixteenth centuries.

The seventeenth century witnessed four important hygienic developments in the heads: the advent of seats-of-ease, fore turrets, roundhouses, and pissdales. Between 1670 and 1680, distinct individual sanitary accommodations, or seats-of-ease, placed within the structure of the head and equipped with trunking, or drainage sluices, made their first appearance on models, although we have archaeological evidence from the *Wasa* of 1628. Fore turrets, devices seemingly peculiar to the French, debuted and quickly disappeared, although they may have left an enduring legacy. In combination with the imitation of semicircular head galleries (e.g., on the *Charles* of 1668), fore turrets may have helped bring about the appearance of roundhouses. These were "perhaps the most satisfactory form of convenience found in ships. Access was through a door in the [beakhead] bulkhead, there was often a small port for ventilation and light, and presumably the occupant was left in a solitary state."[1] The same cannot be said of another seventeenth-century development, the pissdale. This was a convenience installed at the head and amidships that consisted of a simple urinal trough plumbed with lead pipes extending directly through the platform of the head or through the sides of the ship. It was designed for, and experienced, heavy traffic, without regard for solitude or protection from the elements.

During the eighteenth and nineteenth centuries, an increase in the relative area of the head platform allowed for more gratings, a greater number of freestanding necessary seats, and the arrangement of grouped, multihole conveniences placed against the forward-most part of the bow. About the middle of the nineteenth century, radical changes in bow designs were brought about by the introduction of iron-hulled ships. These changes so affected the sanitary accommodations at the bow that they were necessarily moved amidships.

Of all the types of hygienic conveniences developed at the bow over the course of some five hundred years, only the roundhouse survived into the twentieth century, and that in a modified form.

Amidships

Steep- or necessary tubs, when depicted, seem to have been moved from the sterns and quarters to the main chains of either or both sides of the hull about 1550. Early in the seventeenth century, they are seen in association with angular side-shelves, but necessary tubs are not represented in the pictorial record after this brief appearance. Similarly, side-shelves, whose development may have resulted from the shift of garderobes from the quarters to the main chains, were depicted throughout the seventeenth century and became rare in the art of the 1700s. After the removal of the "heads" to positions amidships in the mid-nineteenth century, multihole platforms, which resembled devices formerly used at the bow, can be understood to have been a resurrected, if altered, form of the side-shelf of the 1600s.

The use of pissdales continued unabated from their initial appearance in the last half of the seventeenth century until the end of the nineteenth. Indeed, until the mid-twentieth century they saw service as crew's urinals placed amidships and plumbed through the bulwarks directly into the sea.

The Stern

The employment of three primary external hygienic accommodations located in the sterns of fifteenth-century ships has been suggested: (1) barrel-like attachments on the stern quarter and over the transom and counter, often called steep-tubs after their alternate, though it is hoped mutually exclusive, food-preparation function; (2) closetlike additions over the counters that projected from the sterncastle, similar to garderobes in contemporaneous castle architecture; and (3) structures that closely resembled castle turrets and probably performed much the same function. Small projections through the counters, which may have been soil-pipes or plumbing from facilities within the sterncastle, have been noted but are not here considered a major feature. In fact, they probably were used in one form or another in conjunction with the three types of stern facilities of the fifteenth century.

In the course of the sixteenth century, steep-tubs were moved to the main chains and garderobes to the quarters, where the walls of the sterncastle were still relatively flat, in stark contrast to the multi-countered, sharply raked overhanging sterns that were the fashion. However, garderobes disappear from the pictorial record after about 1525 and are not seen again until the early seventeenth century, by which time they had been moved to the fore end of the open quarter galleries, introduced in the 1530s. Quarter galleries remained largely open through the remainder of the 1500s, but the first third of the seventeenth century witnessed their increasing enclosure, a development that may have gained some impetus from the placement of the garderobe on the quarter. The remainder of the 1600s was a period of grand-scale decorative elaboration, readily apparent on the quarter galleries of ships of the time.

Throughout the eighteenth and most of the nineteenth centuries, hygienic accommodations at the stern remained virtually unchanged. Quarter galleries with one, two, and occasionally three levels remained the principal conveniences for senior officers. But by the fourth quarter of the nineteenth century, quarter galleries had been eliminated because of the advent of iron-hulled ships and attendant major changes in stern designs.

It appears that early flushing water closets were first installed in the quarter galleries of British ships of the line in 1779. However, they do not seem to have been used extensively until well into the 1800s; by that time, the conveniences were internal, that is, placed within the fabric of the hull.

Appendix

BIBLIOGRAPHIC ESSAY

Sources of information for this study include contemporary pictorial representations, ship models, and descriptive accounts of voyages at sea; secondary historical treatments of voyages; general works on seafaring, ships and their construction, and life at sea; histories of medicine and sanitation, nautical medicine, and naval hygiene; and archaeological reports. Regarding privies, latrines, and so on, from terrestrial contexts and, more specifically, human waste removal from sailing vessels or any accommodations on them that facilitated this action, there is a severe dearth of literary information.

By far the most important sources are a number of contemporary depictions, as there seem to exist far more illustrations of external sanitary accommodations than descriptions. Perhaps this fact lends veracity to the material, in that the artists were not sacrificing realism to societal mores or modesty.

Several prints by the famous unknown Flemish marine artist who signed his works "WA" are the best sources for mid- to late fifteenth-century vessels, especially carracks. Other artists of a similar school have provided depictions of Italian, Spanish, French, and English ships of the fourteenth, fifteenth, and sixteenth centuries. Without doubt, the most comprehensive repositories of these illustrative materials are the early volumes of the *Mariner's Mirror*, the journal of the Society for Nautical Research. Certain authors tended to write argumentative, serial-like articles in which a good deal of ego was involved. Yet the figures included in these highly informative volleys were often excellently rendered and, with few exceptions, accurate. Perhaps the most prolific contributor during this period was R. Morton Nance. For over forty-five years, he wrote knowledgeably about a variety of subjects. I have either cited or consulted some twenty-three of his articles regarding fifteenth- and sixteenth-century ships alone.

Certain maritime-oriented Dutch masters (e.g., Brueghel, Van de Velde the Elder and Younger, and Broom) are the best sources for seventeenth-century illustrations. Publications that contain these sketches and paintings include *Sailing Ships*, *The Ship of the Line*, and *Great Ships: The Battlefleet of King Charles II*.[1]

Illustrative evidence for the mid-seventeenth to nineteenth centuries consists largely of drawings of contemporary ship models in the collection of the National Maritime Museum, Greenwich, as presented in the single best literary source consulted, J. Munday's "Heads and Tails: The Necessary Seating."

Additional sources for this period include various paintings, etchings, woodcuts, tapestries, and ship models that I have examined in the major maritime museums of Europe. The holdings of the National Maritime Museum in Greenwich, the Scheepvaart Museum and the Rijksmuseum in Amsterdam, and the Musée de la Marine in Paris have all been gleaned for evidence of external sanitary accommodations. Iberian institutions in which I have conducted hygienic research include the Museo Naval, Madrid; the Archivo General de Indias in Seville; the Museo Marítimo, Barcelona; and the Museu da Marinha in Lisbon.

Perhaps the relative absence of contemporary descriptions of hygienic conditions in general, and sanitary facilities in particular, is due in part to social strictures, an aversion to discuss basic bodily functions, acceptance of the relatively unhealthy environments common throughout the period, and general ignorance of the specific associations among filth, germs, and disease. J. H. Parry offers an additional, simpler explanation for the lack of "details of life at sea," particularly during the fifteenth and sixteenth centuries: "Sailors were practical men, little given to writing. Explorers kept journals, but rarely troubled to include information about a daily round which to them was familiar, and which they took for granted. The best accounts of ships' routine and conditions on board ship were written by landlubbers who, for one reason or another, made sea voyages as passengers."[2]

Subsequent editions and translations of these landlubbers' accounts have been examined.[3] Though enlightening because of the pictures they paint of maritime life, they have yielded few, if any, specific details regarding waste-disposal practices and conditions below decks. In one outstanding description of a voyage from Spain to the New

World in 1573, written by Eugenio de Salazar and republished, after translation, in a collection entitled *The European Reconnaissance: Selected Documents*, the trials and tribulations involved in the usually simple act of defecation are cynically addressed: "If you want to relieve yourself . . . you have to hang out over the sea like a cat-burglar clinging to a wall. You have to placate the sun and its twelve signs, the moon and the other planets, commend yourself to all of them, and take a firm grip of the wooden horse's mane; for if you let go, he will throw you and you will never ride him again. The perilous perch and the splashing of the sea are both discouraging to your purpose, and your only hope is to dose yourself with purgatives."[4]

From this and other tidbits in this narrative one can glean a few helpful scraps of information about accommodating the human need under such circumstances: that it was necessary to "hang out over the sea" in order to accomplish the task, that one was often "splashed" by the seas, and that there was some reliance on laxatives. However, there are no decipherable clues as to exactly where on the vessel these daring deeds took place, or to the structural features of the ship (if any) that facilitated their accomplishment. Perhaps de Salazar was referring to "hanging out" from the lee fore or main chains (Fig. 6.2). This seems always to have been a viable alternative in all but the worst weather.[5] With respect to aiding the reconstruction of the material culture of shipboard life and the vessels of the time, particularly their sanitary facilities, such a lack of detail is a characteristic shortcoming in the available literature.

General works on seafaring, ships, and ship construction provide extremely useful contemporary depictions and illustrations and occasionally address the subject of sanitary facilities in general terms.[6]

Historical treatments of nautical medicine and naval hygiene and sanitation are revealing but disappointingly general in their approach to the matter.[7]

A number of publications deal with waste disposal and sanitary facilities in terrestrial contexts, but only one article has been found to date that forthrightly addresses the nautical aspects of the issue.[8] Although generally excellent, its usefulness is somewhat limited because sanitary facilities only aboard English ships from the late seventeenth to mid-nineteenth centuries are discussed.

Another source of information is evidence from underwater archaeological contexts. Scant but enlightening clues from preserved organic remains and artifacts encountered in and on the ballast piles

Fig. 6.2. "Hanging out" from the fore chains. (Drawing by David Macaulay.)

and within the bilges of shipwrecks from the period are coming to light.[9] As far as is known, only one component of what was probably an external sanitary accommodation has been discovered in an archaeological context: a lead plumbing pipe presumably from one of the bow latrines of the *Dartmouth*.[10] In the interest of completeness,

however, it should be noted that an oddly shaped length of lead pipe—
probably the basin of the head and uppermost segment of downward-
projecting trunking—was recovered from the wreck of the *Whydah*
by treasure salvagers.[11] A wooden basin found on the wreck of HMS
Fowey might have served as a urinal or pissdale but probably was not
externally mounted.[12]

Notes

Chapter 1. Introduction

1. Marsden 1975, 125.
2. Ballard 1944, 67.
3. Pudney 1954, 80.
4. Gray 1974, pl. 1; Karageorghis and des Gagniers 1974, 122.
5. Marinatos 1973, 292; 1974, 50.
6. DeVries and Katzev 1972, 42, fig. 5.
7. Casson 1971, figs. 151, 154.
8. van Doorninck 1991.
9. Porphyrogenitus 1830, 671A; van Doorninck 1982.
10. Morison 1971, 135.
11. Compare Holt 1892.
12. Martin 1978, 34.
13. Peterson 1955, 2.
14. Lloyd and Coulter 1961, 12; Roddis 1941, 116.
15. Peterson 1972, 264.
16. Allison 1942, 15.
17. Falconer 1780, 177.
18. Liou 1974, 423; Fitzgerald and Raban 1989, 188.
19. Martin 1978, 34.
20. Adams 1983.
21. Price and Muckelroy 1977, 193, 195, 198; Muckelroy 1978, 177.
22. de la Torre 1973, 471.
23. Parry 1968, 351.
24. Fox 1980, 21.
25. de la Torre 1973, 469.
26. Marsden 1975, 51.

27. Allison 1942, 19; Cameron 1973, 155.
28. Lloyd and Coulter 1961, 71–72.

Chapter 2. The Fifteenth Century

1. Howard 1979, 14.
2. Arenhold 1911, 299.
3. Nance 1913c, 35.
4. Ibid.; Nance 1912e, 176; 1955, 187.
5. Nance 1913c, 35.
6. Fliedner 1985, 12–13; Kiedel 1985, 76, 77, ill. 66, drawing on inside front cover.
7. Kiedel 1985, 77–78, ill. 67; Keweloh 1991.
8. Nance 1911c, 336.
9. Laughton 1974, 104.
10. 1914d, 277.
11. Nance 1911c, 336; 1955, 180.
12. Howard 1979, 22.
13. Laughton 1974, 31; Howard 1979, 22.
14. Nance 1955, 284, 288.
15. Ibid., 189–90.
16. Ibid., 288–89; Laughton 1961, 102.
17. Jones 1979, 93; Howard 1979, 22; Nance 1911d; Smith 1652, 37.
18. de Groot and Vorstman 1980, pl. 3, caption.
19. Nance 1955, 284.
20. Ibid.
21. Bowen 1951, 190.
22. Jones 1978, 46.
23. Howard 1979, 27.
24. 1966, 31.
25. 1975, 156.
26. Harris and Lever 1966, 38.
27. Nance 1912d, 229.
28. Ibid.
29. Harris and Lever 1966, 7; Thompson 1975, 235.
30. Thompson 1975, 156.
31. 1975, 235.
32. Laughton 1974, 219.
33. 1913d, 69.
34. Ibid., 245.

Chapter 3. The Sixteenth Century

1. Laughton 1974, 31; Nance 1924, 212–13.
2. Laughton 1974, 33, 34.
3. Ibid.
4. Ibid., 41–42.
5. Munday 1978, 125.
6. Fernández Duro 1880, 47.
7. Howard 1979, 51, 98.
8. 1974, 171.
9. Keevil 1957, 116.
10. Rule 1983, 148.
11. Casson 1964, 98.
12. Laughton 1974, 161.
13. Nance 1955, 296.
14. Howard 1979, 51, 79, 163, figs. 114, 246.
15. Laughton 1974, 161.
16. Casson 1964, 98.
17. Howard 1979, 51.
18. Ibid.
19. Ibid., 61.
20. Nance 1914b.

Chapter 4. The Seventeenth Century

1. Lavery 1984, 47–48.
2. Laughton 1974, 34–35.
3. Ibid., 35; Lavery 1984, 58.
4. Laughton 1974, 35.
5. Martin 1978, 52, fig. 28.4.
6. Ibid., 37, 53; Muckelroy 1978, 188.
7. Munday 1978, 127; Stevens 1949, 65.
8. Curator Östling (1991) notes, after an inspection of the ship, that there is no evidence of other types of sanitary accommodations aboard the *Wasa*, but that it was, after all, a new ship and perhaps not completely finished.
9. Munday 1978, 127.
10. Ibid.
11. 1652, 36.
12. Munday 1978, 127.
13. Ibid.; Redknap 1976, 288.

14. Anderson 1913a.
15. Howard 1979, 90–91, fig. 127.
16. 1974, 219.
17. Ibid., 53; Anderson 1921, 314.
18. Laughton 1974, 53.
19. Fox 1980, 95, fig. 104.
20. Laughton 1974, 53.
21. W. 1914.
22. Laughton 1925, 27; 1974, 53; Munday 1978, 127.
23. Lavery 1984, 142, fig. 1.
24. 1914b.
25. Laughton 1974, 219.
26. Nance 1914b.
27. Ibid.; Anderson 1914b.
28. Anderson 1914a, 1914b; Howard 1979, 111.
29. Anderson 1921, 312; Howard 1979, 96.
30. Östling 1991, n. 9.

Chapter 5. The Eighteenth and Nineteenth Centuries

1. It should be noted that there were countless idiosyncratic variations and combinations of sanitary facilities on vessels throughout the period. Yet they did not represent a significant departure from earlier practices, and it would serve little purpose to detail them here.
2. Anderson 1921, 312; Laughton 1925, 9.
3. Stevens 1949, 70, 115.
4. 1978, 130.
5. Ibid., 127; Stevens 1949, 70.
6. Munday 1978, 128.
7. Ibid., 131.
8. Ibid., 128, 131.
9. Ibid., 127.
10. Laughton 1974, 53.
11. Munday 1978, 126.
12. Capper 1930, 416.
13. Stevens 1949, 66.
14. Munday 1978, 127.
15. Ibid., 131.
16. Roberts and Roberts 1947, 4–5.
17. Lavery 1984, 141; Goodwin 1987, 215, photo p. 199.

18.   Ballard 1930, 217.
19.   Munday 1978, 133.

Chapter 6. Conclusion

1.   Munday 1978, 127.

Appendix. Bibliographic Essay

1.   de Groot and Vorstman 1980; Lavery 1984; Fox 1980.
2.   Parry 1968, 348.
3.   For example, Carletti 1965; de la Torre 1973; Gage 1928; and Roberts and Roberts 1947.
4.   Parry 1968, 357.
5.   Munday 1978, 131.
6.   For example, Anderson 1921; Artíñano 1920; Casson 1964; Fernández Duro 1880; Howard 1979; Laughton 1974; Lloyd 1968; and Stevens 1949.
7.   Fonssagrives 1886; Gatewood 1909; Holt 1892; Keevil 1957, 1958; Lloyd and Coulter 1961; Roddis 1941; Shaw 1929.
8.   Examples of publications dealing with terrestrial facilities are Holt 1879 and Pudney 1954. The article dealing with nautical facilities is Munday 1978.
9.   Adams 1983; Martin 1978; Muckelroy 1978, 177; Price and Muckelroy 1977, 193, 195, 198.
10.   Martin 1978, 52–53.
11.   Muncher 1988.
12.   Fischer 1986.

Bibliography

Adams, J. 1983. Personal communication, in response to a question after the delivery of a paper about the *Sea Venture* (1607), the Fourteenth Conference on Underwater Archaeology, Denver, Colorado.

Allison, R. S. 1942. *Sea diseases: The story of a great nautical experiment in preventive medicine in the Royal Navy*. London: John Bale Medical Publications.

Anderson, R. C. 1913a. A French warship built in Holland, 1626. *Mariner's Mirror* 3: facing p. 376.

———. 1913b. The *Prince Royal* and other ships of James I (pt. 2). *Mariner's Mirror* 3: 305–307.

———. 1914a. Notes. Side-shelves and entry-ports. *Mariner's Mirror* 4: 153.

. 1914b. Notes. Port. *Mariner's Mirror* 4: 153–54.

———. 1920a. More heresies about decks. *Mariner's Mirror* 6: 329–32.

———. 1920b. The *"Prince Royal"* of 1610. *Mariner's Mirror* 6: 365–68, and five plates following.

———. 1921. Comparative naval architecture. 1670–1720 (pts. 1, 2, 3). *Mariner's Mirror* 7: 38–45, 172–81, 308–15.

Arenhold, L. 1911. Ships earlier than 1500 A.D. *Mariner's Mirror* 1: 298–301.

———. 1913. Notes. Ancient German ships. *Mariner's Mirror* 3: 312–13.

Artíñano y de Galdácano, G. 1920. *La arquitectura naval española (en Madera): Bosquejo de sus condiciones y rasgos de su evolución*. Madrid.

Ballard, Admiral G. A. 1930. British battleships of 1870. The *Bellerophon* and *Hercules*. *Mariner's Mirror* 16: 212–38.

———. 1944. British gunboats of 1875. *Mariner's Mirror* 30: 65–73.

Bonino, M. 1978. Lateen-rigged medieval ships: New evidence from wrecks in the Po Delta (Italy) and notes on pictorial and other documents. *Inter-*

national Journal of Nautical Archaeology and Underwater Exploration 7: 9–28.

Boulind, R. H. 1968. The crompster in literature and pictures. *Mariner's Mirror* 54: 3–17.

Bowen, R. L. 1951. The dhow sailor. *American Neptune* 11: 161–202.

Brindley, H. H. 1911. Mediaeval ships in painted glass and on seals (pts. 3, 4). *Mariner's Mirror* 1: 129–34, 193–200, 250–51.

———. 1912. Mediaeval ships (pts. 5, 6). *Mariner's Mirror* 2: 44–52, 166–73.

Bruce, R. S. 1929. Queries. 34. *Janet. Mariner's Mirror* 15: 319.

Callender, G. 1912. The ships of Maso Finiguerra. *Mariner's Mirror* 2: 294–300.

Cameron, I. 1973. *Magellan, and the first circumnavigation of the world.* New York: Saturday Review Press.

Capper, H. D. 1930. Notes. British battleships of 1870. *Mariner's Mirror* 16: 416–17.

Carletti, F. 1965. *My voyage around the world.* Translated by Herbert Weinstock. London: Metheuen & Co.

Casson, L. 1964. *Illustrated history of ships and boats.* Garden City, N.Y.: Doubleday.

———. 1971. *Ships and seamanship in the ancient world.* Princeton, Mass.: Princeton University Press.

Chapelle, H. I. 1932. Queries. 22. Closed Heads. *Mariner's Mirror* 18: 329.

Crumlin-Pedersen, O. 1972. The Vikings and the Hanseatic merchants: 900–1450. In G. F. Bass (ed.), *A history of seafaring based on underwater archaeology.* London: Thames & Hudson, 181–204.

de Groot, I., and R. Vorstman. 1980. *Sailing ships: Prints by the Dutch masters from the sixteenth to the nineteenth centuries.* New York: Viking Press.

DeVries, K., and M. L. Katzev. 1972. Greek, Etruscan, and Phoenician ships and shipping. In G. F. Bass (ed.), *A history of seafaring based on underwater archaeology.* London: Thames & Hudson, 37–64.

F., C. 1912. Answers. 176. Royal Yacht. *Mariner's Mirror* 2: 60.

Falconer, W. 1780. *An universal dictionary of the marine.* London: T. Caldwell.

Fernández Duro, C. 1880. *Disquisiciones náuticas.* Madrid: Imprenta Estereotipia y Gablanoplástica de Aribau y Compañía.

Fischer, G. 1986. Personal communication.

Fitzgerald, M. A., and A. Raban. 1989. Area Y: Roman shipwreck. In A. Raban (ed.), *The harbours of Caesarea Maritima: Results of the Caesarea ancient harbour excavation project, 1980–1985.* Vol. I, pt. I. *BAR* International Series 491. Greenwich, Conn.: 184–90.

Fliedner, S. 1985. The find of the century in the Weser River: Bremen's Hanse cog: Discovery and identification. In K.-P. Kiedel and U. Schnall (eds.), *The Hanse cog of 1380*. Federal Republic of Germany: Forderverein Deutches Schiffahrtsmuseum e. V., Bremerhaven, 7–24.

Fonssagrives, J. B. 1886. *Tratado de higiene naval*. Madrid: Miguel Finesta.

Fox, F. 1980. *Great ships: The battlefleet of King Charles II*. Greenwich: Conway Maritime Press.

G., S. 1911. Notes. Mediaeval ships. *Mariner's Mirror* 1: 184.

Gage, T. 1928. *The English American: His travail by sea and land*. London. Reprinted in 1958 as *Travels in the new world*. Norman: University of Oklahoma Press.

Gatewood, J. D. 1909. *Naval hygiene*. Philadelphia: P. Blakiston's Son & Co.

Goodwin, P. 1987. *The construction and fitting of the English man of war, 1650–1850*. London: Conway Maritime Press; Annapolis: Naval Institute Press.

Gray, D. 1974. Seewesen. *Archaeologia Homerica* I G: 1–166.

Harris, J., and J. Lever. 1966. *Illustrated glossary of architecture, 850–1830*. New York: Clarkson N. Potter.

Holt, J. 1879. *The evil and the remedy for the privy system of New Orleans*. New Orleans: New Orleans Auxiliary Sanitary Association (New Orleans Medical and Surgical Association).

———. 1892. *An epitomized review of the principles and practice of maritime sanitation*. New Orleans: L. Graham & Son.

Howard, F. 1979. *Sailing ships of war, 1400–1860*. Greenwich: Conway Maritime Press.

Howarth, D. 1977. *Dhows*. London, Melbourne, New York.

The Isle of Thanet Archaeological Unit. 1979. *Wreck of a British man-of-war discovered on the Goodwin Sands*. Interim report. Kent, England.

Jewell, J. H. A. 1969. *Dhows at Mombasa*. Nairobi, Kenya: East African Publishing House.

Jones, A. G. E. 1979. The dangerous voyage of Captain Thomas James, 1631–1632. *Journal of the Royal Naval Medical Service* 65: 93–98.

Jones, V. 1978. *Sail the Indian Sea*. London and New York: Gordon & Cremonesi.

Karageorghis, V., and J. des Gagniers. 1974. *La céramique chypriote de style figuré: Âge du fer (1050–550 av. J.-C.): Illustrations et descriptions des vases*. Rome: Instituto per gli Studi Micenei ed Egeo-Anatolici.

Keevil, J. J. 1957. *Medicine and the navy, 1200–1900*. Vol. I (1200–1649). Edinburgh and London: E & S Livingstone.

———. 1958. *Medicine and the navy, 1200–1900*. Vol. II (1649–1714). Edinburgh and London: E & S Livingstone.

Keweloh, H.-W. 1991. Personal communication with Frederick M. Hocker (April 11).

Kiedel, K.-P. 1985. The life of a sailor in the Hanse period. In K.-P. Kiedel and U. Schnall (eds.), *The Hanse cog of 1380.* Federal Republic of Germany: Forderverein Deutches Schiffahrtsmuseum e. V., Bremerhaven, 74–80.

Laughton, L. G. C. 1924. H.M.S. *Victory:* Report to the *Victory* technical committee of a search among the Admiralty records. *Mariner's Mirror* 10: 173–211.

———. 1925. The study of ship models. *Mariner's Mirror* 11: 4–28.

———. 1961. The square-tuck stern and the gun-deck. *Mariner's Mirror* 47: 100–105.

———. 1974. *Old ship figure-heads and sterns: With which are associated galleries, hancing-pieces, catheads and divers other matters that concern the "grace and countenance" of old sailing-ships.* Reprint of 1925 edition. New York: B. Franklin.

Lavery, B. 1984. *The ship of the line.* Vol. II: Design, construction and fittings. Annapolis: Naval Institute Press. First published in Great Britain by Conway Maritime Press, Greenwich, 1984.

Liou, B. 1974. L'épave romaine de l'anse Gerbal à Porte-Vendres. *Comptes rendus de l'Académie des Inscriptions et Belles-Lettres:* 414–33.

Lloyd, C. 1968. *The British seaman, 1200–1860, a social survey.* 1970 American edition. Cranbury, N.J.: Associated University Presses.

———, and J. L. S. Coulter. 1961. *Medicine and the navy, 1200–1900.* Vol. III (1714–1815). Edinburgh and London: E & S Livingstone.

Marinatos, S. N. 1973. Apollonius argon. A 970. *Athens Annals of Archaeology,* fasc. 2: 289–92.

———. 1974. *Thera VI (1973 Season).* Athens.

Marsden, P. 1975. *The wreck of the Amsterdam.* New York: Stein & Day.

Martin, C. J. M. 1978. The *Dartmouth,* a British frigate wrecked off Mull, 1690. 5. The ship. *International Journal of Nautical Archaeology and Underwater Exploration* 7: 29–58.

Moore, A. 1911. Of decks and their definitions. *Mariner's Mirror* 1: 76–79, 178–82.

———. 1912. A difficult passage and the "naval repository." *Mariner's Mirror* 2: 214–15.

Morison, S. E. 1971. *The European discovery of America: The northern voyages,* A.D. *500–1600.* New York: Oxford University Press.

———. 1974. *The European discovery of America: The southern voyages,* A.D. *1492–1616.* New York: Oxford University Press.

Muckelroy, K. 1978. *Maritime archaeology*. Cambridge: Cambridge University Press.

Muncher, D. 1988. Personal communication.

Munday, J. 1978. Heads and tails: The necessary seating. In *Ingrid and other studies*. Maritime Monographs and Reports, no. 36. Greenwich: Trustees of the National Maritime Museum, 125–40.

Nance, R. M. 1911a. Dutch gable stones. *Mariner's Mirror* 1: 171–78.

———. 1911b. A fifteenth century trader. *Mariner's Mirror* 1: 65–67.

———. 1911c. An Italian ship of 1339. *Mariner's Mirror* 1: 334–39.

———. 1911d. Notes. Shifter. *Mariner's Mirror* 1: 349.

———. 1912a. Answers. 176. Royal Yacht. *Mariner's Mirror* 2: 92.

———. 1912b. Notes. A Cromwellian ship-stern. *Mariner's Mirror* 2: 249–51.

———. 1912c. A sixteenth-century sea monster. *Mariner's Mirror* 2: 97–104.

———. 1912d. Some old-time ship pictures (pts. 1, 2). *Mariner's Mirror* 2: 225–32, 309–15.

———. 1912e. A trader and a man-of-war—late XIV century. *Mariner's Mirror* 2: 174–76.

———. 1913a. The *Ark Royal*. *Mariner's Mirror* 3: 138–42.

———. 1913b. A Hanseatic Bergentrader of 1489. *Mariner's Mirror* 3: 161–67.

———. 1913c. Northern ships of circa 1340. *Mariner's Mirror* 3: 33–39.

———. 1913d. Some old-time ship pictures (pts. 3, 6). *Mariner's Mirror* 3: 65–70, 238–45, 276–79.

———. 1914a. A "Great Dane" of 1600. *Mariner's Mirror* 4: 225–32.

———. 1914b. Notes. An English ship's "side shelf." *Mariner's Mirror* 4: 55.

———. 1914c. Notes. The "*Ark Royal*." *Mariner's Mirror* 4: 154–55.

———. 1914d. Some old-time ship pictures (pt. 7). *Mariner's Mirror* 4: 275–82.

———. 1919. Cromsters. *Mariner's Mirror* 5: 46–51.

———. 1924. Notes. The *Santa Anna*. *Mariner's Mirror* 10: 212–14.

———. 1955. The ship of the Renaissance (pts. 1, 2). *Mariner's Mirror* 41: 180–92, 281–98.

O., D. 1912. Queries. 9. Round House. *Mariner's Mirror* 2: 31.

O'Scanlan, T. 1974. *Diccionario marítimo español* (1831). Madrid: Museo Naval.

Östling, C. 1991. Letter as Curator, VasaMuseet, Stockholm, to Michael A. Fitzgerald (April 3).

Parry, J. H. 1968. *The European reconnaissance: Selected documents*. New York: Walker.

Peterson, M. L. 1955. The last cruise of HMS *Loo*. *Smithsonian Miscellaneous Collections* 131.2: 1–39.

———. 1972. Traders and privateers across the Atlantic, 1492–1733. In G. F. Bass (ed.), *A history of seafaring based on underwater archaeology*. London: Thames & Hudson, 253–80.

Porphyrogenitus, Constantius. 1830. *De Caeremoniis aulae Byzantinae*. Bonn (ed.), vol. 2, chap. 45.

Price, R., and K. Muckelroy. 1977. The *Kennemerland* site: The third and fourth seasons 1974 and 1976: An interim report. *International Journal of Nautical Archaeology and Underwater Exploration* 6: 187–218.

Pudney, J. 1954. *The Smallest Room*. London: M. Joseph.

Redknap, M. 1976. A lavatory seat from Neatham, Hampshire. *Britannia* 7: 287–88.

Rees, A. 1970. *Rees's naval architecture*. Devon, England: David & Charles. Extracts from the first edition, 1819–20.

Roberts, K., and A. M. Roberts (eds. and trans). 1947. *Moreau de St. Méry's American journey [1793–1798]*. Garden City, N.Y.: Doubleday.

Robinson, G. 1920. The development of the capital ship (pt. 2). *Mariner's Mirror* 6: 44–50.

———. 1921. The development of the capital ship (pt. 3). *Mariner's Mirror* 7: 108–17.

Roddis, L. H. 1941. *A short history of nautical medicine*. New York and London: Harper & Brothers.

Rule, M. 1983. *The Mary Rose*. 2nd ed., rev. Greenwich: Conway Maritime Press.

Shaw, T. B. 1929. *Naval hygiene*. London: Oxford University Press.

Sheppard, T. 1939. The old Dutch whalers. *Mariner's Mirror* 25: 50–61.

Smith, J. 1652. *The sea-mans grammar*. London.

Sottas, J. 1912. Guillaume Le Testu and his work. *Mariner's Mirror* 2: 65–75.

Stevens, J. R. 1949. *An account of the construction and embellishment of old time ships*. Toronto.

Thompson, A. H. 1975. *Military architecture in medieval England*. Reprint of the 1912 edition. East Ardsley, England: EP Publishing.

de la Torre, T. 1973. Travelling in 1544 from Salamanca, Spain to Ciudad Real, Chiapas, Mexico: The travels and trials of Bishop Bartolome de Las Casas and his Dominican fathers. Frans Blom (ed. and trans.). *Sewanee Review* 81: 429–537.

van Doorninck Jr., F. H. 1982. Personal communication.

———. 1991. Personal communication.

Vaughan, H. S. 1914. Figureheads and beak-heads of the ships of Henry VIII. *Mariner's Mirror* 4: 37–43.

Verwey, D. 1932. Answers. 34. The *Janet*. *Mariner's Mirror* 18: 98.

W., A. B. 1914. Answers. 9. Round House. *Mariner's Mirror* 4: 158.

Whall, W. B. 1914. The *Great Harry*. *Mariner's Mirror* 4: 65–69.

Index

Note: Pages with illustrations are indicated by italics.

Studies in Nautical Archaeology

Mark, Samuel. *From Egypt to Mesopotamia: A Study of Predynastic Trade Routes,* 1997.

Mott, Lawrence V., *The Development of the Rudder: A Technological Tale,* 1997.

Oertling, Thomas J., *Ships' Bilge Pumps: A History of Their Development, 1500–1900,* 1996.